BEYOND DEATH'S DOOR

collects Dr. Rawlings findings from resuscitating individuals who have been considered clinically dead. He describes the starting point of his work:

"I was resuscitating a terrified patient who told me he was actually in hell. He begged me to get him out of hell and not to let him die. When I fully realized how genuinely and extremely frightened he was, I too became frightened . . . Now I feel assured that there is life after death, and not all of it good."

The book is filled with compelling interviews with the revived and tells how these experiences turned Dr. Rawlings from a man who once considered religion "all hocus-pocus" into a believing Christian.

Included in *Beyond Death's Door* are easily learned, step-by-step cardiopulmonary resuscitation techniques for the layman.

By Dr. Maurice Rawlings, M.D.
Specialist in Internal Medicine
and Cardiovascular Diseases

BEYOND
DEATH'S
DOOR

Maurice Rawlings, M.D.

BANTAM BOOKS
TORONTO • NEW YORK • LONDON • SYDNEY • AUCKLAND

BEYOND DEATH'S DOOR

*A Bantam Book / published by arrangement with
Thomas Nelson Inc., Publishers*

PRINTING HISTORY

Thomas Nelson edition published July 1978
2nd printing .... August 1978   4th printing ... October 1978
3rd printing .. September 1978   5th printing .. November 1978
6th printing ... February 1979
Serialized in The Sydney Evening Sun, *Australia, Fall 1978*
Bantam edition / September 1979
9 printings through August 1987

*Unless otherwise indicated, Scripture quotations are from the
New American Standard Bible, copyright © The Lockman
Foundation 1960, 1962, 1963, 1968, 1971, 1972, 1973, 1975, and
are used by permission.*

Scripture quotations marked TLB are from The Living Bible
*(Wheaton, Ill.: Tyndale House Publishers, 1971) and are used
by permission.*

*Bantam Books are published by Bantam Books, Inc. Its trade-
mark, consisting of the words "Bantam Books" and the por-
trayal of a rooster, is Registered in U.S. Patent and Trademark
Office and in other countries. Marca Registrada. Bantam
Books, Inc., 666 Fifth Avenue, New York, New York 10103.*

CONTENTS

CONTENTS

To my own cross,
The cause of my undoing
And the reason for my salvation.

ACKNOWLEDGMENTS

I want to thank each person who had a part in writing this book. The after-death experiences reported herein were not chosen to support a particular faith or philosophy, but when they did involve scriptural or historical issues, expert opinions were sought in those fields.

I would like to thank in particular Rev. Matthew McGowan, minister of the Central Presbyterian Church in Chattanooga, for his inspirational sermons and continued encouragement to me in the completion of this book. Equally inspiring was Rev. Ben Haden of First Presbyterian Church whose critical comments and individual tutorship helped me compose and present this message in writing. The scriptural intent, content, and application in this book were critiqued by Kay Arthur and her staff at Reach Out, Inc., of Chattanooga. Organization and continuity were patiently monitored by Peter Gillquist of Thomas Nelson Publishers.

My sincere gratitude goes to the persistent efforts of Dr. Bert Bach, dean of arts and sciences at the University of Tennessee at Chattanooga for his grammatical and structural corrections and historical knowledge. The verbal support and expert typing of my secretary at the Diagnostic Center, Mrs. Ella McMinn, is certainly appreciated, along with the back-up support of her enthusiastic young associate, Mrs. Toni Chappell. Library assistance was through the reference department of Chattanooga's Bicentennial Library. Without these people, and without the patience of my family, this book would not have been possible.

MAURICE S. RAWLINGS, M.D.

Diagnostic Center
Chattanooga, Tennessee
March 1978

INTRODUCTION

What is more important to you than your own life? Does death represent the end of your life or the beginning of another? Does anyone know what happens after death? Has anyone been there? What does it feel like?

Public interest in these questions continues to grow as more people survive the death experience through modern restorative techniques called *resuscitation,* which involves breathing for the patient and maintaining his heartbeat until he can recover his own functions. Some of these patients give us rather startling descriptions of an immediate "life beyond." After those pleasurable experiences, the victim often loses his fear of death.

Many people have wondered why recently reported experiences all seem to be good ones. They have asked why after-death experiences do not also represent unpleasant, or bad, experiences.

As a cardiologist exposed to critically ill patients in the coronary care units of several hospitals, I have had many opportunities to resuscitate people who have clinically died. I have found that an interview immediately after patients are revived reveals as many bad experiences as good ones. It is this observation that led to the conception of this book, which will enlarge upon the after-death experiences of several patients and present both the good and bad experiences for the reader's own evaluation. I will also be drawing upon my personal teaching experience and American Heart Association research to present new techniques for restoration of life.

Since being promoted to the National Teaching Faculty of the American Heart Association in 1976, I have had the unusual opportunity of talking to doctors, nurses, and ambulance personnel in many countries, including the Netherlands, Finland, Russia, and Central and South America. In addition, I have had the privilege of lecturing in several medical schools in the United States and to many other groups of physicians, dentists, nurses, and paramedical technicians. Many of these people were kind enough to supply a great amount of comparative material from their own personal experiences with their own patients. Apparently the experiences of patients retrieved from death are being reported by doctors and nurses all over the world now that new resuscitative techniques and advanced support measures are being used by emergency medical services.

Renewed interest in the phenomenon of death and in related subjects seems to be an international trend in the medical profession. The subject is now being popularized, and is captivating the thoughts of the American public. Many seminars and publications dealing with death, the dying process, and life after death are now available.

Before gathering material for this book, I personally regarded most after-death experiences as fantasy or conjecture or imagination. Most of the cases I had heard or read about sounded as if they represented euphoric trips of an anoxic mind. Then one evening in 1977 I was resuscitating a terrified patient who told me he was actually in hell. He begged me to get him out of hell and not to let him die. When I fully realized how genuinely and extremely frightened he was, I too became frightened. Subsequent cases with terrifying experiences have burdened me with a sense of urgency to write this book. Now I feel assured that there is life after death, and not all of it is good.

Detailed accounts of on-the-scene resuscitation events will be reviewed in the ensuing chapters. I shall endeavor to create in the reader a personal awareness of another world into which I was accidentally thrust. Out of this unintentional exposure, I shall attempt to recapture the experiences of patients who were clinically dead and to sort out and explain some of the different types of death, including those that are reversible and those that are irreversible.

Data will be presented for the reader's own evaluation and thought, including some ancient experiences of life after death with illustrations of comparative similarities to present-day findings. The remarkable repetitive sequence of events and parallel experiences in completely unrelated cases seem to exclude the possibility of any coincidence or connecting circumstances during this out-of-the-body existence.

Included in case reports will be some baffling instances of recall of specific events that actually occurred in the confinement of the room during the period of clinical death and complete unconsciousness. The events are so minutely and accurately recounted by the patient as to suggest a spiritual existence outside the body during this period of clinical death. Several notable people in past history have recounted similar experiences although the descriptive literature is meager.

Contemplation of death will be a subject dealt with separately; it is important to distinguish this matter from the actual death experience. Individuals, when informed of their impending death, may experience varying visions, apparitions, or emotions that are sometimes difficult to evaluate objectively although such experiences have been extensively documented. Recorded after-death experiences, on the other hand, have great similarities in the portrayed sequence of events and, therefore, lend themselves quite readily to comparative analyses.

The purpose of this book, therefore, is to recount the experiences of individuals who have survived clinical death and returned to life to tell us about it. Of those who are retrieved from death by restarting the heartbeat and breathing, only about twenty percent volunteer experiences of a life beyond. These patients return to tell us that death, a distressful thought to the average person, does not represent finality or oblivion, but instead a graduation from one life into another—an existence sometimes gratifying and in other instances terrifying. When the experience is pleasurable, these people assure us that the death process itself is painless—a simple faint, a missed heartbeat—like going to sleep.

Although death is a certainty for us all, man still refuses to accept the inevitability of death. He is displeased with this threat to his assumed immortality, a confirmation that he may actually lack assurance of another life.

BEYOND
DEATH'S
DOOR

1

TO HELL AND BACK

More and more of my patients who are recovering from serious illnesses tell me there is a life after death. There is a heaven and a hell. I had always thought of death as painless extinction. I had bet my life on it. Now I have had to reconsider my own destiny, and what I have found isn't good. I have found it really may not be safe to die!

The turning point in my own thinking occurred because of the event I alluded to previously. I requested that a patient perform what we call a "stress test" to evaluate complaints of chest pains. In this test we exercise the patient and simultaneously record the heartbeat. A treadmill machine paces the patient's exercise so that he slowly builds up to a jog, then to a run. If the heart record (EKG) goes "haywire" during the exercise, we can usually be sure the patient's chest pains originate in the heart, explaining the source of his "angina pectoris," or pain in the chest.

This patient was a forty-eight-year-old white male who was a rural mail carrier. He was of medium build, dark haired, and had a personality that would please anyone. Unfortunately, he represented one of those rare instances where the EKG not only went "haywire," but the heart stopped altogether. He had a cardiac arrest and dropped dead right in my office. Instead of fibrillating (twitching without a beat), the heart had just plain stopped. He crumpled to the floor, lifeless.

With my ear to his chest, I could hear no heartbeat at all. With my hand alongside his Adam's apple, I could feel no pulse. He gave one or two sighing breaths before he quit breathing altogether. There were scattered muscle twitchings and then convulsions. He was gradually turning blue.

Although six other doctors work as partners in the same clinic, it was late afternoon and they had gone on to other hospitals to make evening rounds. Only the nurses were left. But they knew what to do and their performance was commendable.

While I started external heart massage by pushing in on his chest, one nurse initiated mouth-to-mouth breathing. Another nurse found a breathing mask, which made it easier to expand his lungs for him. Still another nurse brought the emergency cart containing pacemaker equipment. Unfortunately, the heart would not maintain its own beat. A complete heart block had occurred. The pacemaker was needed to overcome the block and increase the heart rate from thirty-five beats per minute to eighty or one hundred per minute.

I had to insert a pacemaker wire into the large vein beneath the collarbone which leads directly to the heart. One end of this electric wire was manipulated through the venous system and left dangling inside the heart. The other end was attached to a small battery-powered gadget that regulates the heartbeat and overcomes the heart block.

The patient began "coming to." But whenever I would reach for instruments or otherwise interrupt my compression of his chest, the patient would again lose consciousness, roll his eyes upward, arch his back in mild convulsion, stop breathing, and die once more.

Each time he regained heartbeat and respiration, the patient screamed, "I am in hell!" He was terrified and pleaded with me to help him. I was scared to death. In fact, this eipsode *literally* scared the hell out of me! It terrified me enough to write this book.

He then issued a very strange plea: "Don't stop!" You see, the first thing most patients I resuscitate tell me, as soon as they recover consciousness, is "Take your hands off my chest; you're hurting me!" I am big and my method of external heart massage sometimes fractures ribs. But this patient was telling me, "Don't stop!"

Then I noticed a genuinely alarmed look on his face. He had a terrified look *worse* than the expression seen in death! This patient had a grotesque grimace expressing sheer horror! His pupils were dilated, and he was perspiring and trembling—he looked as if his hair was "on end."

Then still another strange thing happened. He said, "Don't you understand? I am in hell. Each time you quit I go back to hell! Don't let me go back to hell!"

Being accustomed to patients under this kind of emotional stress, I dismissed his complaint and told him to keep his "hell" to himself. I remember telling him, "I'm busy. Don't bother me about your hell until I finish getting this pacemaker into place."

But the man was serious, and it finally occurred to me that he was *indeed* in trouble. He was in a panic like I had never seen before. As a result, I started working feverishly and rapidly. By this time the patient had experienced three or four episodes of complete unconsciousness and clinical death from cessation of both heartbeat and breathing.

After several death episodes he finally asked me,

"How do I stay out of hell?" I told him I guessed it was the same principle learned in Sunday school—that I guessed Jesus Christ would be the one whom you would ask to save you.

Then he said, "I don't know how. Pray for me."

Pray for him! What *nerve!* I told him I was a doctor, not a preacher.

"Pray for me!" he repeated.

I knew I had no choice. It was a dying man's request. So I had him repeat the words after me as we worked—right there on the floor. It was a very simple prayer because I did not know much about praying. It went something like this:

> *Lord Jesus, I ask you to keep me out of hell.*
> *Forgive my sins.*
> *I turn my life over to you.*
> *If I die, I want to go to heaven.*
> *If I live, I'll be "on the hook" forever.*

The patient's condition finally stabilized, and he was transported to a hospital. I went home, dusted off the Bible, and started reading it. I had to find out exactly what hell was supposed to be like. I had always dealt with death as a routine occurrence in my medical practice, regarding it as an extinction with no need for remorse or apprehension. Now I was convinced there was something about this life after death business after all. All of my concepts needed revision. I needed to find out more. It was like finding another piece in the puzzle that supports the truth of the Scriptures. I was discovering that the Bible was not merely a history book. Every word was turning out to be true. I decided I had better start reading it very closely.

A couple of days later, I approached my patient with pad and pencil in hand for an interview. At his bedside I asked him to recall what he actually saw in hell. Were there any flames? Did the devil have a pitchfork? What did hell look like?

He said, "What hell? I don't recall any hell!" I recounted all of the details he had described two days earlier while he was on the floor next to the treadmill machine being resuscitated. He could recall none of the unpleasant events! Apparently, the experiences were so frightening, so horrible, so painful that his conscious mind could not cope with them; and they were subsequently suppressed far into his subconscious.

The man, by the way, has stayed "on the hook." He is now a strong Christian, although before this incident he had gone to church only occasionally. Although he is too shy and reticent to speak before groups, he has remained a compelling personal witness for Jesus Christ on a one-to-one basis. He does, however, remember the prayer we said and he remembers "passing out" once or twice after that. He still does not recall the experiences that occurred in hell, but he does recall standing in the back of the room and watching us work on his body there on the floor.

He also recalls meeting both his mother and stepmother during one of these subsequent death episodes. The meeting place was a gorge full of beautiful colors. He also saw other relatives who had died before. This experience was very pleasurable, occurring in a narrow valley with very lush vegetation and brilliant illumination by a huge beam of light. He "saw" his mother for the first time. She had died at age twenty-one when he was fifteen months old, and his father had soon remarried. This man had never even seen a picture of his real mother, and yet he was able to pick her picture out of several others a few weeks later when his mother's sister, after hearing of his experience, produced some family pictures for identification. There was no mistake. The same auburn hair, the same eyes and mouth—the face was identical to the lady he saw in his experience.

She was still twenty-one years old. There was no doubt it was his mother. He was astounded and so was his father.

Similar circumstances may explain the paradox of finding only "good cases" reported in the literature thus far. When patient interviews are delayed in any way, this may allow enough time for the good experiences to be mentally retained and reported by the patient and the bad experiences to be rejected or obliterated from recall.

Future observations should confirm these findings as emergency room physicians and those physicians routinely exposed to critical-care medicine develop the courage to investigate spiritual matters through on-the-scene interviews with patients immediately after their resuscitation from clinical death. Since only about one-fifth of those resuscitated have experiences to report, many such interviews may prove fruitless. When experiences are found, however, they are like finding gems that would previously have been cast away as useless. Such "gems" have convinced me, beyond a shadow of a doubt, that there is life after death and that not all of it is good.

There is more to the story of this particular patient. His true heart condition was exposed by the episode of cardiac arrest that occurred in my office. After he recovered, chest pains persisted that were out of proportion to those expected from the manual compression of the chest wall during heart massage.

Coronary catheterization (a procedure for examining the heart vessels) permitted visualization of the abnormal arteries on the heart wall that were causing his trouble. Since the coronary arteries are usually too small to permit removal of the obstructing material, blood vessels have to be taken from the leg and implanted on the heart surface above and below the obstructed arteries to serve as "bypass" grafts. Our surgical team was called in for this procedure.

As a cardiologist, my responsibility includes the catheterization, diagnosis, and treatment but not the surgery. But on this particular occasion, I joined the surgical team of several doctors and operating technicians. The combined conversation both at the operating table and previously at the catheterization table went something like this:

"Isn't that interesting," one doctor said to the others. "This patient said he was in hell while he was being resuscitated! But that actually doesn't concern me too much. If there is a hell, I don't need to worry. I've led a respectable life and I've always taken care of my family. Other doctors may run out on their wives, but I never have. I also look after the children and I'm putting them through school. So I don't have to worry. If there is a heaven, I'll get there."

What this first doctor said I knew was wrong, but I couldn't quote the Scriptures that might indicate the reasons. I looked them up later and discovered there were plenty.[1] I just *knew* you couldn't get there by being good.

Further conversation across the table was continued by another doctor. "I don't believe there is any life after death. I think this patient just imagined that he was in hell. There really is no such place." When I asked him what basis he had for this belief, he replied, "I was in seminary for three years before I entered medical school. I left seminary because I couldn't bring myself to believe that there is a life after death."

"What do you think happens to a person after he dies?" I asked.

---

[1] John 3:3; 3:16; 14:6; Prov. 14:12; Isa. 64:6; Rom. 10:9.

"When a person dies, he becomes fertilizer for the flowers," was his answer. He was serious, and he still believes that.

I am ashamed to say that I, too, was just as guilty. In fact, I was worse than the others. One of the doctors who loves to needle me was trying to amuse the others with this question: "Somebody told me, Rawlings, that you were baptized in the Jordan River. Is that true?"

I tried to avoid the whole question by changing the subject. Instead of saying something simple like "Yes, it was one of the happiest days of my life," I sidestepped the issue. I changed the subject, which was the same as denying it! I have regretted that decision ever since. And I continue to recall the passage where Jesus said if we deny Him before men He will deny us before His Father in heaven (see Matt. 10:33). I hope my insignias are more visible now.

The point of relating this conversation is to underscore our need for missionary work at home. In addition to sending Christians overseas, perhaps we should also send them to the operating rooms of our local hospitals!

Let me again emphasize that contrary to most published life-after-death cases, not all death experiences are good. Hell also exists! After my own realization of this fact I started collecting accounts of unpleasant cases that other investigators apparently had missed. This has happened, I think, because the investigators, normally psychiatrists, have never *resuscitated* a patient. They have not had the opportunity to be on the scene. The unpleasant experiences in my study have turned out to be at least as frequent as the pleasant ones. Is the Bible then true? The answer soon became personally compelling—and one to share for the evaluation of you, the reader.

2

BRING 'EM BACK ALIVE

We in the medical trade spend much of our time dealing with death—preventing it if we can and retrieving people from it whenever possible. We have a word for this method of bringing them back alive: *resuscitation.*

Before we get into actual life-after-death reports, I am going to devote this chapter and the next to a discussion of two basic areas that will help you to better understand the after-death experiences themselves. This chapter will be given over to resuscitation: how it works and its relationship to the experiences of the dying patient. Then, in Chapter 3, I want to focus in on why we die and some specific things we all can do to keep our bodies healthy.

I have taught resuscitation methods to others for about fifteen years. The methods outlined in this chapter will help you to respond effectively to the sudden death of a companion. Whereas old methods were rarely successful, continued new refinements in resuscitation can now bring restoration of life to *greater than fifty percent of all sudden deaths* not involving cata-

9

strophic injury. Without any equipment and using one's bare hands, anyone with minimal training can use these techniques with some success. *Resuscitation* is the art of inducing breathing with your breath and simulating heartbeat with your hands. Resuscitation is a most ingenious and simple way to bring the clinically dead back to life.

Death as experienced prior to resuscitation is difficult to define and understand. Strange encounters may occur during such experiences. Reversible death (or clinical death) is that type of death that is potentially recoverable by restarting the heart and lungs. The brain and underlying vital tissues have not yet died; when the brain and vital tissues die, irreversible death (or tissue death) has occurred. Resuscitation from reversible death should certainly not be confused with *resurrection* from irreversible death. One requires training; the other a miracle!

Almost everyone will see an unexpected sudden death during his lifetime and therefore should know how to restore the victim to life. There is no time to wait for help from others.

BASIC RESUSCITATION TECHNIQUES

Resuscitation consists of artificially induced respiration and circulation.

Respiration is accomplished by mouth-to-mouth breathing, which is administered manually by closing off the patient's nostrils while forcing your air into his lungs through his mouth. When properly done, the unconscious victim's chest will expand with air. Exhalation of this air automatically occurs from elastic recoil of the dead person's chest when you momentarily remove your mouth to allow for the next breath.

Circulation is maintained by externally massaging the heart. This is done by placing the heel of one hand on the lower portion of the breastbone and the other hand on top of that hand, and pressing down to squeeze the heart between the yielding breastbone in front and the rigid backbone behind, simulating a heartbeat.

The cycle is interrupted after every fifteen compressions for two quick breaths into the victim (if you are working alone). Massage time is equally divided between compression and relaxation and sixty to eighty beats per minute are delivered. Since heart valves are designed to flow one way, the heart blood is compressed forward into the arterial blood vessels, and the heart passively refills itself between compressions. If properly done, the pulse can be felt as an expansion in the neck vessel just beside the Adam's apple (the carotid artery). This pulsation will confirm a correct procedure, regardless of the patient's subsequent survival.

No longer is it necessary to surgically open the chest and expose the heart for direct massage. The present method is just as effective for recovery.

Speed and efficiency in administering resuscitation is the key to recovery in these cases of unexpected death. Ninety-eight percent will survive if pulse and breathing are assisted within one minute after death—if within two minutes, ninety-two percent and within three minutes, seventy-two percent. But only fifty percent will survive if four minutes elapse and only eleven percent after six minutes.

AIRWAY OBSTRUCTIONS

Obstructed airways caused by choking or asphyxia contribute to fifty percent of all deaths. Obstruction should be suspected when the patient struggles to get air into his lungs without much success. Sometimes a "crowing" noise can be heard as the patient inhales air past a partial obstruction. Struggling without a noise is a grave emergency indicating a complete obstruction.

Death will occur quickly if not relieved. Subsequent re-suscitation may dislodge the obstructing material, but any resistance encountered when forcing one's breath into the victim's lungs is evidence of continued airway obstruction. Failure of the chest to visibly expand with air further confirms an obstruction.

The most common airway obstruction in the un-conscious patient is due to the relaxed tongue sagging against the back wall of the throat. The patient does not "swallow his tongue," although the concept is compara-ble. Elevating the chin upward and extending the top of the head backward toward the floor (when the pa-tient is lying on his back) will usually permit immediate, smooth and unobstructed breathing. Many uncon-scious patients die due to simple suffocation from an obstructing tongue, which could have been easily cor-rected.

The American Heart Association is attempting to instruct everyone, including our elementary school chil-dren, in how to recognize and treat the obstructed airway. For example, if a child escapes injury in a devas-tating automobile accident with his family, he should know how to elevate the chin of an unconscious family member until the ambulance arrives, preventing death from suffocation.

Other airway obstructions may be due to improp-erly swallowed meat, inhaled food particles, false teeth, or anything that may result in blockage or closure of the vocal cords (laryngospasm). Any obstructions that the patient can't remove through coughing can of-ten be expelled by abdominal or chest-thrust maneu-vers. These are performed by forcefully squeezing in on the lower chest or upper abdomen. Such techniques force air out of the lungs in an attempt to dislodge the material from a critical area of the windpipe into an area of the throat where it can be removed.

Mouth-to-mouth resuscitation may also dislodge

the obstruction. By blowing the foreign material from the windpipe down into one of the lungs, the victim is often able to maintain breathing with the remaining lung. The foreign body can subsequently be removed from the lung at a more convenient time through an instrument called a bronchoscope. The bronchoscope is a hollow tube that is passed through the windpipe into the lung and through which the obstructing material can be grasped with forceps and removed.

I recall the unfortunate story concerning one of three beautiful daughters of Colonel Antonio A. Batres, chief of Guatemala's Air Force. I was flying to Guatemala to deliver some relief supplies and typhoid vaccine that had been donated by fellow physicians in Chattanooga for earthquake victims there. Just a week before the earthquake, Colonel Batres's daughter, who was in her twenties, had gone to see her dentist in downtown Guatemala City. During some dental procedure—it was not clear whether it was a filling or an extraction—she suddenly developed a "wheezing" noise. She couldn't breathe. She turned blue and became unconscious. Having never encountered a case of airway obstruction during his many years of practice, the dentist didn't know what to do. He ran into the streets of downtown Guatemala City yelling "Help! Help!" In the meantime she died. Had he known and followed the basic steps just outlined, her death could have been prevented.

SURVIVAL TIME

In more than one thousand ambulance calls made in response to victims with sudden death (cardiac arrest) in Seattle, it has been found that only eighteen percent can be brought back to life if the public waits for resuscitation by the ambulance crews—who, in this study, took only a few minutes to arrive. On the other hand, the long-term survival rate was more than doubled—with forty-six percent recovering—if the "passersby" instituted immediate resuscitation before the ambulance arrived. This diminished that critical time the patient existed without heartbeat or breath exchange. It is here we need public education.

The brain has only four minutes survival time without heartbeat and blood supply. Even a physician living next door would not do much good for the average victim of heart arrest, be it from heart attack, drowning, electrocution, poisoning, or suffocation. It would be much longer than the four minute survival time before the doctor could possibly initiate resuscitation. It is important that everyone, therefore, become familiar with cardiopulmonary resuscitation (CPR). This training is available in detail through your local chapter of the American Heart Association or Red Cross in almost all cities. I urge you to take it.

Ambulance crews are being authorized to initiate advanced life-support measures at the scene of an emergency rather than waiting to administer such treatment after the patient arrives at the hospital. Advanced life-support measures now include electrocardiograms to detect and treat abnormal heart rhythms, electrical defibrillation shock when necessary, intravenous lifelines for the administration of drugs, insertion of airway devices for controlled breathing, and special methods of transportation.

Many of us can recall observing a case of sudden death. It is not uncommon. I recall the unexpected death of a good friend a few years ago at Calloway Gardens, a plush resort in Georgia. While bicycling at this resort, my friend, who was in his forties, started complaining of "gas" in the center of his chest. It was a first for him. We had flown there to play golf, swapping his lessons in golf for mine in flying. My golf that day was awful (as usual) so the opportunity to bicycle with our wives was a welcome change.

However, his "indigestion" became increasingly painful and spread into his jaws and arms. He decided to lie down on the lawn. The pain got worse, and as he became pale and breathless everyone started gathering around him. Suddenly, he arched his back in a stiff convulsion, sputtered, rolled his eyes upward, stopped breathing, and turned grayish-blue. I started mouth-to-mouth resuscitation with four quick breaths, tilting his head backward for a good airway and closing his nostrils with my fingers. Feeling no pulse and hearing no heartbeat with my ear to his chest, I started external heart massage.

He finally opened his eyes and tried to speak, but each time I interrupted resuscitation he slipped back into a deep coma. Then he would partially awaken again, half-grimacing, half-smiling, and reach for or point at something. I believe he was trying to tell me something, but I didn't take time to listen. I was more concerned with finding any available medications.

During all this time he had no heartbeat of his own, but I was sure he was in ventricular fibrillation (silent twitching). With no monitoring instruments or equipment, I knew I had to continue to maintain resuscitation during the long ambulance trip back to the hospital, where a defibrillator could be obtained.

The ambulance arrived and we lifted him in. It so happened the ambulance did carry a portable defibrillator unit, but it hadn't been checked recently and was found to carry no charge. We stopped at a farm house along the way to plug into their electricity for recharging the defibrillator, but it wouldn't charge. The instrument was useless. When we arrived at LaGrange Hospital almost two hours had elapsed. By that time electric shock treatment proved futile.

Of course, I wonder now what really transpired. What was he trying to say? I missed the opportunity to listen to him during those important moments. I did not ask him what he saw, where he was, or what went on. I have allowed many such opportune moments to escape in the past. But no more!

Of the one-half million Americans who are at risk of dying of heart attack each year (called myocardial infarction), more than 360,000 die before they can reach a hospital. Since most die in the first two hours, sixty percent of patients with acute myocardial infarction never reach a coronary care unit. Most of these early or sudden deaths appear to represent ventricular fibrillation, which is a twitching, non-contracting heart.

If we are to effectively reduce mortality we must inform the public not only of the heavy, squeezing mid-chest pains of heart attack but also of the necessity of early and prompt hospitalization. Present statistics suggest that the elapsed time between onset of complaints and admission into a coronary care unit is appallingly high—estimated at *nine hours* as a national average!

Furthermore, if sudden death occurs in the home or office, the average available person has had no training in resuscitation or is too afraid to use it. By the time qualified help is contacted, the four-minute time limit for brain survival has expired. Perhaps we need to focus more attention on this pre-hospital phase and concentrate on greater education and training of the public.

LIFE AFTER DEATH

Only recently has there been a sufficient number of survivors of reversible, or clinical, death to be worthy of comparative analysis. These recent revelations have stimulated current interest in the subject of life after death.

Unfortunately, only about twenty percent of resuscitated individuals describe an experience outside of the body after death. Others may decline to admit such experiences, especially if their experience included being sent to hell. Many people may be reticent to discuss their personal experiences for fear of being labeled "eccentric" or "strange," or for fear of being ostracized by their friends.

Once the subject of life after death is freely discussed, however, the fears of rejection are often replaced by a sympathetic rapport found by confiding in others with similar experiences. If conditions for discussion are made more favorable, further accumulation of after-death reports can be anticipated. The ability to restore life has opened the door onto this corridor we call death, allowing us to peer through the eyes of others to what may lie ahead.

In summary, let's outline the steps for emergency resuscitation to use until help arrives:

1. Confirm unconsciousness first.
2. Open the airway by tilting the head back and check for breathing.
3. If breathing has stopped, give four quick breaths.
4. Check neck pulse.
5. If no pulse, begin external heart compression by depressing lower half of the breastbone one and a half to two inches rhythmically.
6. Continue uninterrupted cardiopulmonary resuscitation (giving two breaths after every fifteen compressions) until advanced life support is available.

Again let me say that for you to develop confidence in your ability to use CPR techniques, you should take the course (usually consisting of one or two meetings) offered by the American Heart Association or the Red Cross. The appendix to this book also offers a detailed description of modern resuscitation techniques.

3

HOW YOU WILL DIE

One of a doctor's primary concerns is to help his patients understand the most likely *cause* of death they will face.

The illness that befell Charles (the forty-eight-year-old mailman who apparently made a visit to hell) could also happen to any one of us at any time. Since you are vulnerable to many unexpected illnesses or accidents, haven't you wondered what will actually be the cause of your own death? Let me briefly address this subject, concentrating especially on diseases of the heart, since these are our number one killers.

THE NUMBER ONE CAUSE

What will be the most likely cause of your death? Diseases of hardened arteries kill more people than all other diseases put together! It is the bane of our existence. Both your chance and mine of dying with such hardened artery conditions as heart attack, stroke, gangrene of the leg, or any other obstructed artery disease

19

are much greater than dying from cancer, automobile accident, infections, or any other condition.

It is a fact that one in every three males past forty-five years of age in the United States will have a heart attack sometime in his life. "You're as old as your arteries" is considered a true saying, since the longevity of man is often limited by the age and condition of these passages.

If hardened arteries were eliminated from the aging process, perhaps man would once again approach the age of Methuselah. Unfortunately, life's duration is still limited by this disease process for which few inroads into prevention have been discovered. Meanwhile, the outlook for duration of life in relation to most other diseases has progressively improved.

Hardened arteries, also known as *arteriosclerosis* or *atherosclerosis*, represent a progressive narrowing of the *lumen* (or opening of these arteries) due to deposits of organic fat elements and calcium salts in their inner walls. These chemical elements are deposited particularly when large amounts of them are present in the bloodstream. *They are chemically identical to materials found primarily in our rich diets.* We absorb excess amounts of organic fat and mineral salts into our bloodstream where they can then be deposited in our arteries, causing them to "harden."

SOME IMPORTANT TERMS

The material accumulated in our arteries can become so thick that it blocks the artery openings or roughens the slick, super-smooth surface inside our arteries, which in turn will allow clots or stoppages to form. The reduction in channel width causes reduced blood flow to the part of the body supplied by the affected artery. Complete blockage or *occlusion* will result in death of that portion of the organ that is involved, especially if there are no other arteries to help supply that area.

This blockage occurs frequently in the heart or brain. Should the occlusion be by a clot, it is called a *thrombosis*. Should tissue death occur, we add the word *infarction*. This hardened artery process may occur anywhere in the body, causing eye infarction (local blindness), kidney infarction (blood in the urine), myocardial infarction (heart attack), cerebral infarction (stroke), and so on.

The infarcted portion of the organ dies and turns "black and blue" as if struck by a hammer. The dead tissue becomes soft and mushy, but is eventually replaced by tough scar or fibrous tissue as healing takes place. Most of the body's healing is done by formation of scar tissue. Hence, we confine our heart attack patients to bed until this infarcted, softened area of the heart wall is replaced by scar tissue.

With premature activity the heart may be excessively exercised and form a bulge *(aneurysm)*, or worse, a "blowout" can occur through this softened area, like a weak place in the tire of an automobile. Massive bleeding into the chest occurs through this ruptured hole, usually resulting in immediate death. Other complications that are even more likely to occur during this acute phase of heart attack include rhythm disturbances, shock, and actual heart failure.

Since the heart wall is a very thick muscle, it cannot be adequately nourished from the blood it pumps. The heart, therefore, like most other organs in the body, has its own system of small pencil-sized arteries that come down over its surface like a crown or "corona"— hence, the name coronary arteries. As already mentioned, any branch of these coronary arteries may become hardened and narrowed from fat and calcium deposits that thicken the inner lining of the artery, reducing its opening and roughening its smooth inner surface. Too much exercise, increasing the heart rate beyond the blood transport capabilities of the narrowed artery, creates a sensation of tightness in the mid-chest called "angina." Should this roughened artery surface become blocked or occluded, a heart attack results, causing a severe persistent tightness or "squeezing" discomfort in the middle of the chest that the patient usually describes as "indigestion" rather than pain. The pain is almost never located in the left chest or over the heart itself and is never "sharp," contrary to popular belief. Strangely enough, most heart attacks occur while the victim is at rest.

The degree of hardened artery involvement can be visualized relatively painlessly by means of a study called *coronary catheterization*. This involves the introduction of a small hollow tube (*catheter*) into the leg (*femoral*) artery in front of the groin, or into the arm (*brachial*) artery in front of the elbow. Through a needle placed into the artery, the tube is introduced and painlessly advanced within the arteries to a level where the special coronary arteries originate to supply the heart wall.

Since all arteries are ordinarily invisible in X rays, special solutions are injected through the catheter into the coronary arteries to make them visible. The coronary arteries are seen as large, smooth, worm-like structures. If they are diseased or hardened, narrowed areas appear that look as if rubber bands had been placed around them. Blood vessels almost anywhere else in the body can be visualized in a like manner.

Coronary catheterization is a procedure done in selected patients to determine the cause of their chest pain. It is also done in patients with disabling heart pains to determine if they would be relieved by "bypass" surgery. In this surgery an extra vein is removed from elsewhere in the body to serve as an artery. This vein is attached above and below the narrowed coronary artery. Hence the name "coronary by-pass surgery."

WATCH YOUR DIET

Population studies suggest that national diet habits have a close correlation with incidence of hardened arteries in each country. The United States, for instance, has a high incidence of heart attacks, strokes, and diabetic gangrene. Surpassing the United States, however, and first in the world are the Netherlands and Finland.

It is interesting that during World War II, when Nazi Germany occupied the Netherlands and sent the confiscated dairy products to Germany in place of the *Ersatz* bread, the Netherlands was no longer the leader in hardened artery diseases. The United States was! Then, as you can imagine, after the Netherlands was liberated at the end of World War II it gradually resumed its place as the world leader in the incidence of heart attacks, strokes, and diseases caused by hardened arteries.

Recently while on a lecture tour in Finland with the American College of Physicians, I became indirectly involved for the American Heart Association in an outbreak of sudden unexplained deaths in one of the far eastern cities of Finland called "Joensuu," translated "mouth of the river." It seemed that the young as well as the old people were unexpectedly dying in the streets or in their homes from episodes of heart arrest, primarily in the form of ventricular fibrillation. No apparent reason could be found; they just dropped dead. Since most of the public had not been taught emergency resuscitation, none of those who succumbed outside of hospital areas survived.

We arranged for a World Health Organization investigating team to come in after we left to try to determine if this epidemic of heart disease is related to their peculiar diet and smoking habits, the tension of being close to the Russian border, their environmental life-style, or some other factor. Their answer should be forthcoming.

However, we do know that when the hearts of these victims were extracted from the chest at autopsy, they seemed to be of normal size but *covered with fat.* Multiple cross incisions of the coronary arteries were done through this encasing fat. Softened deposits of fat narrowed the inside opening of these arteries. These deposits in the arteries resembled ordinary tooth paste and could be removed with a thumb nail. This soft phase of early hardened arteries is in marked contrast to the cases of advanced hardened arteries that we usually see in older people where calcification has occurred. Calcification converts the soft "tooth paste" to a hard and irreversible "egg shell" disease that causes the arteries to feel hard.

The "softened" phase of hardened arteries could conceivably represent an early and resorbable phase of the disease. It seems to involve young people with an unbelievably high rate of incidence. And it is not just peculiar to the Netherlands and Finland. It is found in our own young people in America.

For instance, a revealing study was done during the Korean War involving our draft-selected and most physically fit boys. Of three hundred of these boys who had died in the battlefields, averaging twenty-two years of age, autopsies showed that this "tooth paste" phase of coronary involvement had already occurred in seventy-seven percent! If our most physically fit soldiers had it, then so did our young men at home.

This means that you and I have it too! A man doesn't suddenly, at the age of forty-five, become the one in three males who will eventually develop heart attacks. One does not start experiencing that exertional mid-chest squeezing pain we call angina, often foreboding a future heart attack, unless trouble has been developing long before the pain begins. Females are not exempt. Those who have passed the age of menopause have lost their immunity. As aging occurs and the ovaries cease to function, the seven to one ratio of heart attacks in males compared to females equalizes.

Population studies in other countries also support these findings. While visiting the Orient several years ago with a group of doctors from the American College of Cardiology, we asked to see the coronary care units. There were none. In place of heart disease, their primary cause of death was cancer of the stomach. Heart attacks and diseases of hardened arteries were rare. We weren't sure whether this was related to their rice diet or to their oriental ancestry. The answer came from another group of doctors doing research in the Chinatown area of San Francisco. Careful records were made of the incidence of heart attacks in the immigrant first-generation Chinese. Then the incidence of heart attacks in the second and third generations of purebred Chinese were compared. The rate of heart attacks increased rapidly with the third generation showing the same high rate as those found in the United States.

The material deposited in hardened arteries shows the identical chemical composition of fats and minerals as found in our "better" food substances. This is especially true of fatty foods, sea foods, and dairy products such as butter, cream, cheeses, fatty meats, cooking oils, shortening, egg yolks, shrimp, and lobster. Those people of affluence with sufficient income to afford the "good life" (if that's what it is) are the most vulnerable. As might be expected, the white collar worker is more subject to heart attacks and strokes than the ditch digger. Whether this is a difference in physical activity or type of diet is still uncertain, although both are probably involved.

Chickens seldom get heart attacks unless butter

(or other foods high in cholesterol) is ground into their daily mash. Even the chickens' own egg yolks will do. Eventually heart attacks will occur. If the offending fat substances (cholesterol and triglycerides) are removed from the chicken's diet before heart attacks start to develop, then the deposits of soft tooth-paste-like material in the coronary arteries seem to resorb and disappear into the bloodstream and heart attacks no longer occur. On the other hand, the advanced "eggshell" phase of hardened arteries found in most of us who are past forty-five years of age has not proved to be resorbable or correctable by experimental reduction of the fat products in our diets.

Hardened arteries, therefore, seem to be the major limiting factor for our longevity and existence and are by far the most likely cause of your death and mine. You've heard it a million times, but if you are serious about living out the fullness of your years, watch out for

cigarette smoking
foods high in animal fats and cholesterol,
extra pounds,
lack of exercise,
diabetes,
high blood pressure, and
mid-chest pain.

The saying is all too familiar—it's your choice. You can pay now, or pay later!

4

CONCEPTS OF DEATH

Life after death has been predicted throughout human history, but until recently any specifics of that life have remained a mystery. A glimpse into the future has been man's dream since his beginning. And now, in our lifetime, sufficient descriptions of a life after death have become available for secular credence.

Yet even with these descriptions, this transition at death, being intangible, is not easily understood. As the antithesis of birth, as the apparent dissolution of something into nothing, death defies a simple definition.

What is death? What is this mystery that is visible to us all and is still unanswered and not understood by our greatest scientific minds?

Both the events at death and the stages of death are debatable. Also debatable is the chosen time to stop our efforts of recovery of the victim. Clinical (reversible) death is said to occur when the heart stops and breathing ceases; biological (irreversible) death occurs when all tissues degenerate beyond any function; legal death occurs when the body shows no response to adequate resuscitative efforts. Although biological death would appear to be the end of all existence, man has been peculiarly endowed with the expectation of immortality since the beginning of time. So perhaps a biblical definition of death should be sought. One such definition is that the body is dead when the spirit leaves it: "Just as the body without the spirit is dead . . ." (James 2:26).

Of course, scientific proof for the documented existence of life after death is impossible unless we can produce cases actually resurrected from a biological death where tissues had decayed. As far as I know, this has not occurred since biblical days when Elijah brought back the widow's son (1 Kings 17:17-24) and later the Shunammite's son (2 Kings 4:32) and then when the prophet Elisha was resurrected (2 Kings 13:20). In the New Testament Jesus Himself resurrected three persons: Jairus's daughter (Mark 5:21-24), the son of the widow Nain (Luke 7:11-15) and Lazarus (John 11:1-44). Of course, Jesus's own resurrection after three days of death, is the reason we celebrate Easter.

There are many descriptions that suggest a separation of the spirit from the body at the very onset of death, with the spirit later re-entering the body in the cases of reversible death. Of course, in cases of irreversible death, excluding biblical resurrection, the spirit has never been known to re-enter the body, which suggests that the Scriptures were referring to a biological type of death when man was appointed "to die once, and after this comes judgment" (Heb. 9:27).

Perhaps this also suggests why a specific judgment experience was not described in the case histories of those surviving reversible death. Those who returned to life believing that there is no final judgment may have been deceived. "And no wonder, for even Satan disguises himself as an angel of light" (2 Cor. 11:14). In any event the expectation of another life beyond that door we call death is now typified in case reports such as this:

> I remember getting out of my body head-first and floating over to the corner of the room. My wife was crying and I tried to tell her to look over here at me, that I was all right. But she wouldn't look at me. No one paid any attention. I moved past the two doctors and looked down at my body. The clothes had been burned from the fire and my face was a mess of peeling burnt skin.
>
> The doctor said "Is the machine charged to four hundred?" and then he put two metal discs on my chest that were wired to the machine. I saw my body jump. It was then that I knew I had returned into my body. The pain felt like a mule had kicked me in the chest. This life was certainly worse than the other. I can still remember every detail.*

Belief in life beyond the grave is common in nearly all cultures. As one studies the history of man it is almost impossible to find a people who did not have faith in some form of existence after death.

When man was created the Scriptures indicate that God planted the sense of eternity into the hearts of men: ". . . he has also set eternity into their heart . . . " (Eccl. 3:11). This hope of immortality acts as a "homing" instinct that is so deeply rooted that it has caused man to seek his Creator throughout the ages, perhaps just as homing instincts cause migrating birds, whales, and other animals to accurately seek their own refuge.

---

* Here and elsewhere throughout the book, notably Chapters 6 and 7, the accounts that do not have an accompanying footnote are from interviews with resuscitated patients conducted by me or one of my colleagues.

PRE-BIBLICAL ERA

Belief in life after death was expressed in various ways thousands of years ago. Ancient societies buried their dead with flowers, suggesting that they saw death as an occasion of celebration—perhaps as a transition from this world to the next. They also buried their dead with weapons of war or with food or other provisions for the next life.

The *Egyptian Book of the Dead*, perhaps the oldest piece of literature in the world, is an extraordinary collection of prayers and formulae for guidance in the next world. The Egyptians were apparently the first culture to teach immortality of the soul. The bodies were carefully prepared, dressed, and embalmed; and their personal ornaments, toiletries, weapons, tools, and pots and dishes containing food and drink were placed in the tomb. Life after death was thought to require sustenance in the same way we presently require it—in the form of food and drink.

Their tombs represented their future homes. The higher the earthly rank, the greater the tomb. The great pyramids of the pharaohs, a wonder of the world, still exist as an awesome reminder of the ancient beliefs in life after death. The tombs in which they were buried antedate by more than a thousand years the inscriptions recorded in the *Egyptian Book of the Dead*, which itself dates somewhere around 2500 B.C. The Egyptians, like the vast majority of men throughout history, considered death an interruption of life, not its end.

The Tibetan Book of the Dead outlines life after death as believed by the Orientals of many centuries ago. These beliefs were apparently not recorded in book form until the eighth century A.D. The book describes the art of dying and contains lengthy descriptions of the various stages of the soul after physical death. According to this Tibetan account, at the time of death a person finds that his dead body is left behind and replaced by a "shining" body capable of going through objects and walls without encountering resistance. Travel is instantaneous. At first he notices his friends and relatives lamenting his death and preparing his body for the funeral. In this new state of the released soul, his senses are sharpened and intensified, and he may encounter other spiritual beings, or he may meet a "clear light" that creates feelings of immense peace and contentment. However, he is eventually judged and sentenced, based on his deeds during his physical existence. Other journeys of the soul and stages of death are discussed in this book.

The Babylonians also had a conception of existence beyond the grave. They believed in the resurrection of the dead, including judgment and punishment. They also buried their dead with containers for food and drink, and men were buried with their tools of trade and women with their combs and cosmetics.

The Persians believed that when the soul left the body, it crossed over the Bridge of the Gatherer where, for three days, the spirits of good and evil struggled for possession of the soul. If the good spirits won, the man passed into the boat of song; if the evil spirits won, he fell into the abyss of the "house of hell."

The Greeks contributed more to the world of thought than nearly all other cultures. They believed that death was only the mortal end of man and that the soul remained immortal. The Greek poet Findas believed that some souls returned to earth as wise men. The Greek philosopher Plato taught that the soul separates from the body at death and, being freed from the dead body, meets and talks with other departed spirits, usually relatives or friends. He believed this usually took place in a brilliant environment which the soul eventually had to leave to face the "judgment." At this time all things he had done in his past life were displayed before him.

Similar thoughts were described by Socrates, the famous Athenian philosopher. When facing his own death he was convinced that his soul would "depart to that place which is, like itself, invisible, divine, immortal and wise . . . and where . . . it really spends the rest of time with God." When asked where he wished to be buried, Socrates employed his immortal words, "Bury me if you can catch me," implying that he would no longer be residing in his body.

In *The Republic* Plato described how Er, a Greek soldier who was killed in battle, saw his own body about to be burned on a funeral pyre. He realized his soul had gone out of the body. He then found himself in a place where there were barriers or "openings" leading from the earth to an afterlife. At these openings the souls were interrogated and judged by divine beings after first reviewing all earthly events that had occurred during life. Some spirits would find the column of light illuminating the entrance to heaven, while others found they were cast into hell. Er, however, was not judged at this time, but was returned to his physical body. He woke up on the funeral pyre but left it able to relate this amazing story. Plato then admonished his readers: "Wherefore my council is that we hold fast ever to the heavenly way and follow after justice and virtue always considering that the soul is immortal and able to endure every sort of good and every sort of evil."[1]

Thucydides, a contemporary of Plato from Greece, wrote the history of the Peloponnesian War. He included an oration that Pericles had delivered as the eulogy for the Athenian soldiers who died in the first engagements of the war. There was no reference to

---

[1] Edith Hamilton and H. Cairns, eds., *The Collected Dialogues of Plato* (New York: Bollingen Foundation, 1961).

immortality. Instead, there was an indication that personal sacrifice for the state bestowed a kind of deathlessness upon the soldier. The good of the state was the purpose of existence.

A similar doctrine is taught today in the communist countries. Every day the Soviet people can be seen filing by Lenin's tomb just outside the Kremlin walls in order to see their founder, the "god" they seem to worship. The body has been so well preserved that Lenin really looks as if he could come alive and breathe again at any moment. The thought is intriguing. The body of Mao Tse-Tung is also reported to be in a similar state of preparation for the Chinese people.

OTHER OPINIONS

Beliefs expressed in other cultures concerning life after death have many similarities. Some tribes in Central Africa believe in a spiritual existence after death. The widow frequently takes up residence near the tomb in order to "watch" the departed spirit of her husband. American Indians once resembled the Egyptians concerning their belief in an afterlife. They buried their dead in special mounds with bow and arrow for use in the "happy hunting grounds" in the next life. The Hindu believes in a type of heaven where pearls and jewels exist on the banks of rivers, and flowers and music and laughter and happiness are abundant. The Buddhist, in most of the sects, describes a beautiful paradise at death. The pleasure is universal. The length of life is immeasurable, and the name of "hell" is unknown. Total self-dependence, they believe, leads to salvation, and this state is reached through a series of reincarnations. The Muslims believe in an afterlife where paradise exceeds anything in this world. They believe it is a place of luxury and pleasure promised only to those who follow Allah.

To summarize this nearly universal belief in immortality, let me quote Marcus Porcius Cato, the Roman philosopher who lived before Christ:

> *It must be so. Plato, thou reasonest well:*
> *Else whence this pleasing hope,*
> *This fond desire,*
> *This longing after immortality?*
> *Of whence this secret dread, and inward horror*
> *Of falling into naught?*
> *Why slinks the soul*
> *Back on herself and startles at destruction?*
> *'Tis the divinity that stays within us:*
> *'Tis Heaven itself that points out an here-after,*
> *And intimates Eternity to man.*[2]

THE CHRISTIAN ERA

Just as our calendar is separated by Christ's birth, so are history and the debates of philosophy. The Christian culture's view of death and immortality still parallels the ancient, but adds the missing link of the Creator's revelation of Himself to His creation in the form of man.

In about A.D. 177 Irenaeus, the bishop of Lyons in Gaul, preached that the soul exists after being separated from the body at death. Quoting the New Testament, he taught that body, soul, and spirit compose the whole man.

The Phoenix, a fourth-century Latin poem by Lactantius, maintains that man left paradise because of sin but may regain paradise through the promise of the resurrection. Death is defined as separation of the body and the soul, but these two entities are eventually reunited at the resurrection. God the Creator of the soul,

---

[2] Joseph Addison, *Cato*, Act V, Scene I. Drury Lane, 1713 (Reprinted 1976 by Scholarly Publishers).

provides only one way of redemption: through Jesus Christ.

The majority of modern Christians assumes a fundamental doctrine of the immortality of the soul. We find in 2 Corinthians 5:6-9:

> . . . realizing that every moment we spend in these earthly bodies is time spent away from our eternal home in heaven with Jesus. We know these things are true by believing, not be seeing. And we are not afraid, but we are quite content to die, for then we will be at home with the Lord. So our aim is to please him always in everything we do, whether we are here in this body or away from this body and with him in heaven (TLB).

Paul also made similar assurances to the Philippians:

> But if living will give me more opportunities to win people to Christ, then I really don't know which is better, to live or die! Sometimes I want to live and at other times I don't, for I long to go and be with Christ. How much happier for me than being here! (Phil. 1:22, 23, TLB.)

It is interesting that all of my patients who reported a continuance from one life to another, whether it was good or bad, usually met previous loved ones in a type of sorting place that often had a barrier preventing entrance into a more permanent type of existence. The "light" they saw frequently represented a brilliant environment, while in other instances it seemed to be an angelic being. Satanic-like beings usually were not described in terms of light but in terms of darkness. Of course, we must remember that all descriptions, whether "good" or "bad," were made by the patients themselves and therefore influenced by their cultural backgrounds.

How we interpret what they saw, however, will be heavily influenced by our own commitment to biblical truth or our private beliefs.

SEEING IS BELIEVING

Paul made it clear in the Scriptures that Christians are freed from sin and death by Jesus Christ:

> For I delight in the law of God, in my inmost self, but I see in my members another law at war with the law of my mind and making me captive to the law of sin which dwells in my members. Wretched man that I am! Who will deliver me from this body of death? Thanks be to God through Jesus Christ our Lord! (Rom. 7:23–25.)

If as Christians we have been liberated from sin by Jesus Christ, why is death so abhorrent to most of us? Perhaps it is because we are experiencing the present (human, natural) life and know its reality, but the presence of another (supernatural) life remains unseen and untried by us. We must accept it on *faith*, faith in the promise of God in the Scriptures. Unless we have been born of God, such trust is impossible to achieve.

However, like finding a piece of Noah's Ark, which helps verify the scriptural account of the flood, we now have available some personal testimonies of people who have died and entered the next life, and then have returned to tell us about it. Their accounts have become startling revelations! According to these reports there is a good place and a bad place. Could the Scriptures possibly be true? Suppose the Bible is not just a history book. If the Bible is true, then Jesus Christ really had a first-hand experience: He returned to life by resurrection. He returned to life from a complete biological and irreversible death!

For most of us seeing is believing. Usually we won't buy a commodity until we see it. But we *will* buy it if one of our friends has already used it.

So when people ask me how I know about life after death if I myself have never been there, I give them the answer Dr. Ross H. Stover of Philadelphia gives in his lectures on life after death: "No, I have never been there. But I have a very dear Friend who has been there—Jesus Christ. And I am simply repeating what this Friend told me."

TWO UNSOLVED DILEMMAS

Concerning *birth* and *death*, the two unsolved mysteries of science, man still seeks to be the final judge. Limited in his understanding and experience by his five physical senses, man compared to God is little better than an insect. His world exists for only a small distance in any direction, and yet he considers his opinion enlightened in all directions.

The following example is not that of one of my own patients, but of one who was temporarily resuscitated by a physician from California:

> At the height of his success no one could have known he was so despondent. He told me he was searching for more than life had to offer. I didn't understand him myself. I should have listened, because that night I was called to his home in Beverly Hills and found him on the floor with a bullet wound through his mouth. He revived to consciousness and responded to resuscitation for awhile before he died. I asked him if he hurt. He shook his head no. I told him we were going to try to save him. He nodded in agreement. His last words were, "I'm scared. Don't let me go back to hell. I can see it now." I don't know what he saw.

Since we cannot see the immortal spirit depart from the body at death we assume the spirit does not exist, for our own comprehension of reality is limited by our five bodily senses: what we can see, feel, hear, smell, and taste.

THE REALM OF THE SPIRIT: SOME OBSERVATIONS

If we don't see it, we say it doesn't exist. And even if we do see we may not understand: ". . . because seeing they do not see, and hearing they do not hear, nor do they understand" (Matt. 13:13). This has been one of my own problems.

Yet many people who have experienced clinical death tell us of seeing themselves actually separate from their dead bodies into spiritual form, and then wonder why we can't hear them talking to us. As mentioned before, they are perturbed that everyone in the room keeps looking at the dead body and cannot see the "real" them. The "departed" person can see and hear the people in the room but cannot be seen or heard in return. Apparently you and I are "blinded" to this spiritual world in our present life.

Perhaps this is why, when we visualize a body at death, we assume that the person who occupied that body has also died when actually that "person" has moved on from the body, leaving the body lifeless.

Solomon seems to have described well his concept of death for a believer when the body returns to dust "and the spirit will return to God who gave it" (Eccl. 12:7). The metamorphosis of the caterpillar into the butterfly may be another parallel of a complete transition of life from one form into another, from something common into something beautiful, from something that is earthbound into something that is *un*bound.

The Book of Genesis says man was made from

dust. "Then the Lord God formed man of dust from the ground, and breathed into his nostrils the breath of life; and man became a living being" (Gen. 2:7). Hence, the origin of the funeral oration, "ashes to ashes, dust to dust."

The Bible has much to say about the origin and destiny of man, subjects for which science can find no answers. The body ages and decays, returning to dust. But the spirit, created by God, lives on. The Book of Daniel mentions restoration of our bodies from dust at the resurrection: "Many of those who sleep in the dust of the ground will awake, these to everlasting life, but the others to disgrace and everlasting contempt. And those who have insight will shine brightly like the brightness of the expanse of heaven, and those who lead the many to righteousness, like the stars for ever and ever" (Dan. 12:2,3).

Isaiah had a similar message concerning man's origin and afterlife. Molded by God out of the dust, we shall return to dust, but with this assurance:

"Your [God's] dead will live; Their corpses will rise. You who lie in the dust, awake and shout for joy!

For your dew is as the dew of the dawn . . ." (Isa. 26:19).

Of course, these passages deal with the separation of body and spirit at death and the subsequent resurrection of man into a new form, reuniting the spirit with a new body. Thus the Old Testament deals more with the *resurrection,* while the New Testament deals with *everlasting life.* Paul emphasizes the location of a Christian's spirit when death occurs: to be absent from the body is to be present with the Lord (see 2 Cor. 6-8). Jesus told the repentent thief on the cross that he would be with Him in paradise, not next week or next year, but "today" (see Luke 23:43).

Death in stark reality, however, is not beautiful. The undertaker's most clever handiwork cannot make it attractive. At death, the body becomes an empty corpse, the abandoned protoplasm where someone once lived, a cold, lifeless carcass awaiting return to the dust from which it came. This thing of death is startlingly real. It is the great leveler, the respecter of no man. Reprieve cannot be bought. It cannot be earned. Each of us will come within its grasp.

It seems paradoxical, therefore, that those who have truly found life are less afraid of death than those who live shallowly. If we cannot give meaning to our present life, then death also will be empty and meaningless, and we will not have lost much by the exchange.

None of us knows our appointed time with death. The years go by swiftly and, when we take account, our visit here seems short indeed. Paul has cautioned us, ". . . it is already the hour for you to awaken from sleep; for now salvation is nearer to us than when we believed; the night is almost gone and the day is at hand" (Rom. 13:11, 12). Other scriptural passages emphasize the time limitations of this life and warn of our regrets if life is not well spent. Psalm 90 reads:

> For all our days have declined in Thy fury;
> We have finished our years like a sigh.
> As for the days of our life, they contain seventy years,
> Or if due to strength, eighty years.
> Yet their pride is but labor and sorrow;
> For soon it is gone and we fly away (vv. 9,10).

Job puts it more strongly:

> Man who is born of woman,
> Is short-lived and full of turmoil.
> Like a flower he comes forth and withers.
> He also flees like a shadow and does not remain
> (Job 14:1,2).

And stronger still, Job says:

> . . . *I am decaying like a rotten thing.*
> *Like a garment that is moth-eaten* (Job 13:28).

Encouragingly, Christian teaching is less about death and more about life. There is nothing so important to a person than his own life. Contemplating one's death, therefore, is to understand how to live well. Shakespeare's Hamlet meditates upon the comparative disadvantages of being dead or alive by the phrase, "to be or not to be." A similar question is asked in the Book of Job, perhaps the oldest book in the Bible: "If a man dies, shall he live again?" (Job 14:14.) Job answered his own question in a later passage:

> *As for me, I know that my Redeemer lives*
> *And at the last He will take His stand on the earth;*
> *Even after my skin is flayed,*
> *Yet without my flesh I shall see God;*
> *Whom I myself shall behold.*
> *And whom my eyes shall see, and not another*
> (Job 19:25–27).

For a Christian, even though death has a fearful face for each of us, death can be swallowed up in the assured victory of a life beyond. For Christ has been there, conquering all forms of death and promising us a new life beyond the grave: "because I live, you shall live also" (John 14:19).

5

STRANGE ENCOUNTERS
OF THE LAST KIND

Life after death can be either the enigma or the hope of mankind. Recent on-the-scene interviews of patients returning from clinical death who have experienced transitions into another life reveal that good and bad reports are about equally divided in number. One patient may recall death as wonderful and edifying, while another may suppress his experience because of its destructive or embarassing nature.

We shall present some of the "good," the "bad" and the "odd" after-death encounters in the next several chapters. But before discussing some strange encounters both past and present, let's review a typical out-of-the-body experience.

TYPICAL OUT-OF-THE-BODY EXPERIENCE

The following is an aggregate example from which several variations may occur:

A dying person simply faints or painlessly loses consciousness as death occurs, and yet he is still able to hear himself pronounced dead by his doctor. He then discovers that he is out of his own body, but still in the same room, looking on as a bystander and observing the procedures. He watches himself being resuscitated, and frequently is compelled to walk around other people who might be obstructing his view. Or he may look down upon the scene from a floating position near the ceiling in which he sometimes finds himself. Often he is standing or floating behind the doctor or the nurse, looking down on the back of their heads as they work to revive his body. He notices who is in the room and knows what they are saying. He has difficulty believing that he is dead, that the lifeless body used to be his. He feels fine! The body has been vacated as if it were a strange object.

After he becomes more accustomed to this odd condition he notices that he has a new body which seems real and endowed with superior senses. He is not a ghost. He can see and feel and think and talk just as before. But now fringe benefits have been added. He notices his body has infinite capabilities of transportation and thought-reading, and is capable of doing almost anything. He may then hear a peculiar noise after which he finds himself moving through a long, dark passage with walls. His speed may be fast or slow but he doesn't touch the walls and is not afraid of falling. As he emerges from the tunnel he may see a brilliantly lighted environment of exquisite beauty where he meets and talks with friends and relatives who have previously died. He may then be interviewed by a being of light or a being of darkness. This environment may be inexpressibly wonderful, frequently a rolling meadow or a beautiful city; or it may be inexpressibly horrible, frequently a dungeon or a huge cave. His whole life may be played

44

back as an instant review of all the major events of his life, as if anticipating a judgment.

As he walks along with his friends or relatives (frequently his parents in a good experience), a barrier is usually encountered beyond which he cannot go and still return. He usually is turned back at this point and suddenly finds himself back in his body where he may feel the shock of an applied electric current or chest pains from someone pushing upon his chest.

These experiences usually affect a person's life and attitudes profoundly. If the experience is pleasant, one is not afraid to die again. A person might look forward to renewing this experience where he left off, especially since he has discovered that death itself is painless and presents no fear. If he tries to tell his friends about this experience, he may receive ridicule or quips. Finding the words to describe these unearthly episodes is difficult enough; but if ridiculed, he may keep the episode a secret and say no more. If it is unpleasant, an experience of damning incrimination, he may prefer to leave the story untold.

The terrifying experiences may be as abundant as the pleasant ones. As with those who have had good experiences, those reporting bad experiences may have trouble realizing they are dead as they watch people work on their dead bodies. They may also enter a dark passage after leaving the room, but instead of emerging into bright surroundings they enter a dark, dim environment where they encounter grotesque people who may be lurking in the shadows or along a burning lake of fire. The horrors defy description and are difficult to recall. Compared to pleasant experiences, exact details are difficult to obtain.

It is important to interview people who have died immediately upon resuscitation, while they are still in trouble and calling for help and before the experience can be forgotten or concealed. These strange, negative encounters profoundly affect their future life and their views of death. *I have not seen one such person remain agnostic or atheistic!*

PERSONAL OBSERVATIONS

Let me tell you how I began my study of after-death experiences. I began following published reports of Elisabeth Kubler-Ross (finally compiled in her book *On Death and Dying*[1]) and Dr. Raymond Moody's reports in *Life After Life*.[2] Except for cases of attempted suicide, all of their published reports represented unbelievably good experiences. I couldn't believe this! Their case reports were too pleasant, too euphoric to be true, I thought. As a youth I had been taught there was a "good place" and a "bad place," a heaven and a hell. After the experience of resuscitating a man who said he was in hell and my subsequent belief in scriptural truth, I assumed that some would go to the "bad place." But almost all of these case reports spoke only of a "good place." It then occurred to me that some of the "good" experiences could have been false impressions, perhaps created by Satan appearing as an "angel of light" (see 2 Cor. 11:14). Or perhaps the meeting place is a pleasant environment representing "sorting ground" or a pre-judgment area, since most cases report a barrier that prevents progress into the beyond. The patient returns to his body before the barrier can be transversed. However, a few unusual cases report that they were allowed to break through that "barrier" into what appeared to be heaven or hell. These will be described later.

---

[1] Elisabeth Kubler-Ross, *On Death and Dying* (New York: The Macmillan Co., 1969).
[2] Dr. Raymond Moody, *Life After Life* (Covington, Ga.: Mockingbird Books, 1975).

As a result of these observations, I am convinced that all of the cases published by Dr. Raymond Moody and Dr. Kubler-Ross, and subsequently by Drs. Karlis Osis and Erlendur Haraldsson in their excellent collection *At The Hour Of Death*,[3] are accurately reported by the authors but not always completely recalled or reported by the patients. I have found that most of the bad experiences are soon suppressed deeply into the patient's subliminal or subconscious mind. These bad experiences seem to be so painful and disturbing that they are removed from conscious recall so that only the pleasant experiences—or no experiences at all—are recollected. There have been cases of the patient "dying" several times, with the heart stopping whenever resuscitation was interrupted and consciousness was restored as breathing and heartbeat resumed. The patient in those instances may have had several out-of-the-body experiences. However, he will usually remember only the pleasant details.

It then occurred to me that Dr. Kubler-Ross, Dr. Moody, and other psychiatrists and psychologists were interviewing patients who had been resuscitated by *other* doctors several days to several weeks previously. Neither Kubler-Ross nor Moody, so far as I know, has ever resuscitated a patient or had the opportunity of recording immediate on-the-scene interviews. After many interrogations of patients I have personally resuscitated, I was amazed by the discovery that many have bad experiences. If patients could be *immediately* interviewed, I believe researchers would find bad experiences to be as frequent as good ones. However, most doctors, not wanting to be identified with spiritual beliefs, are afraid to question patients about their after-death experiences.

This concept of immediate interviewing was sug-

---

[3] Drs. Karlis Osis and Erlendur Haraldsson, *At the Hour of Death* (New York: Avon Books, 1977).

gested many years ago by a famous psychologist, Dr. W. H. Myers, who stated,

> It is possible that we might learn much upon questioning dying persons on their awakening from some comatose condition, as to their memory of any dream or vision during this state. If there has in fact been any such experience, it should be at once recorded, as it will probably fade rapidly from the patient's supraliminal memory, even if he does not die directly afterwards.[4]

At the outset of my study I began contacting other doctors who have had similar good and bad experiences reported to them so that sufficient authenticated cases could be compared. At the same time, I started exploring case reports from the past.

STRANGE ENCOUNTERS FROM THE PAST

In reviewing the literature, I found that the King James Bible presented a case somewhat suggestive of mouth-to-mouth resuscitation in 2 Kings 4:34. And although centuries old, *The Tibetan Book of the Dead* had its first known recording in the eighth century A.D., and the fascinating similarity of ancient concepts to present-day experiences is truly remarkable. Descriptions are similar concerning the soul's existence outside the physical body and how the soul has the same bodily senses, only further enhanced and intensified. Travel of the soul is also described as instantaneous, arriving anywhere by thought, going through walls, rocks, or other objects without resistance. In a brilliant environment of pure light, it was believed the soul would meet relatives who had previously died. The soul would then be

---

[4] F.W.H. Meyers, *Human Personality and Its Survival of Bodily Death* (New Hyde Park, N.Y.: University Books, 1961) pp. 212–217.

judged, subsequently serving a penalized existence or other appropriate fate.

Next, I examined the reports of Emanuel Swedenborg, a prolific Swedish writer living in the early 1700s. In his original reports, Swedenborg described his personal experiences while outside his body as he himself went through early events of death. During this state of insensibility, he "perceived and retained in memory the things which occurred, and which occur to those who are sustained from the dead, the process of the spirit being disengaged from the body."[5] First he met inquiring angels and spirits who conversed in a universal language where "the speech of an angel or spirit flows first into the man's thought." He noticed his body was still "recognized by his friends and by those whom he had known in the world . . . wherefore they are instructed by their friends concerning the state of eternal life. . . ." All of the things he had "spoken and done (were) made manifest before the angels, in a light that is clear as day . . . and . . . there is nothing so concealed in the world that is not manifest after death."[6]

More meaningful to me, however, is the detailed report of a physician who, in 1889, went four hours without recorded pulse and thirty minutes without detectable respiration during a coma produced by fulminating typhoid fever. This was recorded in the November 1889 issue of the *St. Louis Medical and Surgical Journal* concerning a Dr. Wiltse of Skiddy, Kansas, treated by a Dr. S. H. Raynes. After Dr. Raynes noted that the gasping respirations of the previous hours had ceased for a full thirty minutes, and that the patient had been without detectable heartbeat for four hours, he

---

[5] Emanuel Swedenborg, *Compendium of the Theological Writings of Emanuel Swedenborg*, Selected by Samuel M. Warren, N.Y., 1974, pp. 591–592.
[6] *Ibid.*

was pronounced dead and the village church bell was tolled. Recalling his own death, Dr. Wiltse reported:

> I came again into a state of conscious existence and discovered that I was still in my body, but that the body and I had no longer any interests in common. I looked in astonishment and joy for the first time upon myself. . . . with all the interest of a physician, I beheld the wonders of my bodily anatomy, [realizing that he was the living soul of that dead body. He reasoned that] I have died, as men termed death, and yet I am as much a man as ever. I am about to get out of the body. I watched the interesting process of the separation of soul and body. . . . I recollect distinctly how I appeared to myself something like a jelly-fish as regards color and form. [His spirit then emerged and] I floated up and down and laterally like a soap bubble attached to the bowl of a pipe until I at last broke loose from the body . . . where I slowly rose and expanded into the full stature of a a man. I seemed to be translucent, of a bluish cast [and as he turned to leave the room his] elbow came in contact with the arm of one or two gentlemen who were standing in the door. To my surprise, his arm passed through mine without apparent resistance, the severed parts closing again without pain as air reunites. I looked quickly up at his face to see if he had noticed the contact but he gave me no sign, only stood and gazed toward the couch I had just left. I directed my gaze in the direction of his and saw my own dead body. It was lying just as I had taken so much pains to place it, partially upon the right side, the feet close together and the hands clasped across the breast. I was surprised at the paleness of the face. . . . I saw a number of persons sitting and standing about the body and particularly noticed two women apparently kneeling by my left

side, and I knew they were weeping. I have since learned that they were my wife and my sister. . . .

I now attempted to gain the attention of the people with the object of comforting them as well as assuring them of their own immortality. I bowed to them playfully and saluted with my right hand. I passed about among them, also, but found that they gave me no heed. Then the situation struck me as humorous and I laughed outright. . . . I concluded the matter by saying to myself: "They see only with the eyes of the body. They cannot see spirits. They are watching what they think is I, but they are mistaken. That is not I. This is I and I am as much alive as ever."

. . . how well I feel, I thought. Only a few minutes ago I was horribly sick and distressed. Then came that change called death which I have so much dreaded. This has passed now, and here am I still a man, alive and thinking, yes, thinking as clearly as ever, and how well I feel; I shall never be sick again. I have no more to die. And in sheer exuberance of spirits I danced a figure and then turned about and looked in at the open door, where I could see the head of my body in align with me."[7]

He then described himself as being lifted and gently propelled through the air by someone's hands and placed on some road in the sky upon which he walked into three

prodigious rocks blocking the road, at which site I stopped, wondering why so fair a road should be thus blocked, and while I considered what I was to do, a great and dark cloud, which I compared to a cubic acre in size, stood over my head. . . . I was aware of a presence which I

---

[7] F.W.H. Myers, *Human Personality and Its Survival of Bodily Death*, pp. 212–217.

could not see but which I knew was entering into the cloud from the southern side. The presence did not seem to my mind as a form because it filled the cloud like some vast intelligence. . . . (and as the cloud) rested lightly upon either side of my head . . . thoughts not my own entered into my brain.

These, I said, are his thoughts and not mine; they might be in Greek or Hebrew for all the power I have over them but how kindly am I addressed in my mother tongue so that I may understand "all is well." And this Being told me, "This is the road to the eternal world. Yonder rocks are the boundary between the two worlds and the two lives. Once you pass them, you can no more return into the body. If your work is complete on earth, you may pass beyond the rocks. If, however, upon consideration you conclude that . . . it is not done, you can return into the body. . . . I was tempted to cross the boundary line. . . . now that I am so near I wanted to cross the line and stay . . . and advance the left foot across the line. As I did so, a small densely black cloud appeared in front of me and advanced toward my face. I knew that I was to be stopped. I felt the power to move or to think leaving me. My hands felt powerless at my side, my head dropped forward, the cloud touched my face and I knew no more.

Without previous thought and without apparent effort on my part, my eyes opened. I looked at my hands and then at the little white cot upon which I was lying and, realizing that I was in the body, and in astonishment and disappointment, I exclaimed, "What in the world has happened to me? Must I die again?"

I was extremely weak, but strong enough to relate the above experience despite all injunctions to be quiet. . . . I made a rapid and good recovery.

> There are plenty of witnesses to the truth of the above statement, insofar as my physical condition is concerned. Also, to the fact that just as I described the conditions about my body and in the room, so they actually were. I must, therefore, have seen things by some means.[8]

How he survived without apparent vital functions for a full thirty minutes is beyond me.

Only a few cases have illustrated both the contemplation of death and the death experience itself. One of these involved Dwight Moody, a shoe salesman of Chicago who became one of the greatest evangelists in Christian history. On a hot Sunday in New York in August, 1899, he said, "Some day you will read in the papers that Moody is dead. Don't you believe a word of it. At that moment I shall be more alive than I am now. . . . I was born of the flesh in 1837. I was born of the Spirit in 1855. That which is born of the flesh may die. That which is born of the Spirit shall live forever."[9]

Later that year, Moody was near death. On a winter morning, Friday, December 22, 1899, his son Will said he heard Moody in his room across the hall saying, "Earth recedes, heaven opens before me!" Will hurried to his father's room. Moody said, "This is no dream, Will. It is beautiful. It is like a trance. If this is death, it is sweet. God is calling me and I must go. Don't call me back!" Then he began to slip into unconsciousness, complaining of no pain, calling it "bliss."

After the labors of his physician, Moody came to and wanted to know where everyone was. He said he had been out of the world. "I went to the gate of heaven. Why, it was so wonderful and I saw the children!" When asked who he saw, he said, "I saw Irene

---

[8] *Ibid.*
[9] J.C. Pollock, *Moody* (New York: The Macmillan Co., 1963) p. 316.

and Dwight." Then he realized he was near the end and said, "I will stay as long as I can, but if my time is come, I am ready. . . . If God wishes, he could work a miracle. I will get up. Doctor, I can die in a chair just as well as in bed, can't I?"[10]

Moody then received his signal for eternity. Nothing need keep him, he said. The chariot was in the room. Thus Dwight Moody first contemplated death, and then temporarily experienced death, to return after seeing his deceased children and heavenly sights. He died subsequently with apparent serenity and anticipation.

Another historical example of life-after-death involved a pioneer in psychoanalysis, Dr. Carl Jung. He described finding himself in a state of semi-consciousness after a heart attack. The description suggests a transient cardiac arrest. After exiting his body he found himself floating away from earth in a glorious blue light and later standing before a temple, the door of which was surrounded by a wreath of flames. He wrote, "It is impossible to convey the beauty and intensity of emotion during these visions. They were the most tremendous things I have ever experienced—I can describe the experience as only ecstasy of a contemporal state in which the present, past and future are one."[11]

He did not describe a barrier or judgment. Perhaps he didn't stay long enough.

Other reported experiences of death or near-death in the past include those of Thomas Edison, Benjamin Franklin, Elizabeth Browning, Eddie Rickenbacker, and also observations and thoughts of such writers as Louisa Mae Alcott and Ernest Hemingway.

---

[10] *Ibid*, pp. 317–318.
[11] Carl Jung, *Memories, Dreams, Reflections* (New York: Pantheon Books, 1963) pp. 295–296.

STRANGE ENCOUNTERS FROM THE PRESENT

Some of my patients have demonstrated astounding powers of recall, accurately reconstructing the events that occurred during the resuscitation, exactly recalling which procedures we used, and describing what each person said in the room and what type and color of clothes each one wore. Several other visualized events suggest a spiritual existence outside the body during the time of prolonged unconsciousness. Such states of coma sometimes last several days.

One such patient was a nurse. At the hospital one day, I was asked to see her in consultation about her heart because of complaints of recurrent chest pains. She was not in her room, but her roommate said she was either in the X-ray department or was still in the bathroom. I knocked on the bathroom door. Hearing no response, I swung the door open very slowly, hoping not to embarrass anyone who might be there.

As the door swung open, there was the nurse hanging from the coat hook on the back of the bathroom door. She was not very large and so she swung easily with the opening door, suspended from the coat hook by a soft collar used for neck sprains. Apparently she had attached this collar around her neck and then fastened the edge of it over the hook, gradually bending her knees until unconsciousness occurred. No suffocation or choking—just a gradual fainting. The more that faintness occurred, the more she slumped. At death, her face, tongue, and eyes were bulging and swollen. Her face had a dark, bluish tinge. The rest of her body had a death pallor. She had long since stopped breathing.

I quickly unhooked her and laid her full length on the floor. Her pupils were dilated. There was no pulse in her neck and no heartbeat could be heard with my ear to the chest. I started external heart resuscitation while her roommate ran down the hall to get help from the nursing staff.

Oxygen and a breathing mask were substituted for mouth-to-mouth ventilation. The electrocardiogram showed straight line "standstill." No electric shock would have helped. Intravenous sodium bicarbonate and epinephrine were given directly in repeated does while other drugs were added to the intravenous bottle. Continuous drip infusion of medications were given to support the blood pressure and help correct the shock.

She was then taken to the intensive care unit by stretcher, where she remained in a coma for four days. Because of the dilated pupils, it appeared that brain damage had occurred from inadequate circulation during the period of heart arrest. Surprisingly though, after a few hours, her blood pressure started returning to normal. Her urine output increased as adequate circulation of blood was restored, but it was several days before she was able to speak. She eventually regained all of her faculties and returned to work several months later.

To this day she believes she had been in some sort of automobile accident that caused her neck to be sore for so long. Whereas she entered the hospital with severe depression, she has now recovered with no residual depression or suicidal tendency, apparently cured by the prolonged period when the brain had no blood supply!

About the second day after recovery from her coma, I asked her if she remembered anything at all. She said, "Oh, I remember you working on me. You took off your plaid brown coat and threw it on the floor, and then you loosened your tie. I also remember that your tie had white and brown stripes in it. The nurse who came to help you looked so worried! I tried to tell her I was all right. You told her to get an Ambu bag and also an intracath to start an I.V. Then the two men came in with a stretcher. I remember all of that."

Recall with me—she was in deep coma at that particular time, and remained in a coma another four days! At the time I took off my brown plaid coat, only she and I were in the room. And she was clinically dead.

Some who survive reversible death have total recall of any conversation in the room that took place during their resuscitation. Perhaps this is because hearing is one of the last senses to leave the body in death. I don't know. But I should have been more careful in the following case.

An elderly gentleman, seventy-three years old, came into the office complaining of crushing mid-chest pain. He was holding his chest as he walked toward my office. He fell midway down the hall, his head hitting the wall as he fell. He sputtered a breath once or twice and then quit breathing. His heart had already stopped.

We pulled his shirt up and listened to his chest to make sure. Artificial breathing and artificial heartbeat were begun mechanically. The electrocardiogram was attached and showed ventricular fibrillation. Each time we applied electric shock through the paddles, the body jumped in response. Afterwards he would arouse, fight us off, climb halfway to his feet, and then suddenly fibrillate again and fall to the floor, often striking his head again. This happened about six times.

Oddly enough, on the sixth time, after several other intravenous supporting medications were given, the shocking procedure held and effective pulse was maintained, blood pressure was restored, consciousness recovered, and the patient is living today. He is eighty-one years old. He got married again following this incident and subsequently managed to get divorced, losing his fruit stand in the bargain, his primary means of livelihood.

Of the six recurrences of clinical death he experienced in my office that day, he recalls only one thing. He recalls me telling the other doctor working with me,

"We'll try one more time. If the shock doesn't hold this time, let's quit!" I wish I hadn't said that because he heard me even though he was completely unconscious at that time. Later he said to me, "What did you mean, 'We'll quit'? That was *me* you were working on!"

HALLUCINATIONS

Oftentimes, people have asked me if these good and bad experiences might not represent hallucinations induced by the severity of the patient's illness or by drugs administered during that illness. Wouldn't it be more likely, for instance, that people see what they wish to see in their visions? Perhaps they are influenced by cultural or religious training? Are the reported experiences truly universal or only visions? Do people with different religious backgrounds, for instance, have similar or dissimilar experiences?

In response to this problem, Dr. Karlis Osis and his associates[12] initiated two studies in America and one in India. Questionnaries were received from over one thousand doctors and nurses who were particularly exposed in their work to dying patients, and the following results were recorded:

1. Those patients taking either sedatives or drugs that are known to produce hallucinations were *less* likely to have after-death experiences than those who took no medications at all. Drug-induced hallucinations, moreover, characteristically pertain to the present world and not to visions of another world or existence.

---

[12] Karlis Osis and Erlendur Haraldsson, "Deathbed Observations by Physicians and Nurses: A Cross-Cultural Survey," *The Journal for the American Society of Psychical Research.*

2. Illnesses that produce hallucinations, such as uremia, chemical poisoning, or brain damage, are associated with fewer encounters with an afterlife or its components than are other diseases.

3. Patients having experiences in an afterlife did not see heaven or hell in the form they had previously conceived. What they did see was usually unexpected.

4. These visions did not appear related to wishful thinking and did not seem to determine which patients would have the experiences. Such visions or experiences would appear as frequently to a patient who had all expectations of recovery as to those who knew they were dying.

5. The sequence of the experience was not altered by differences in culture and religion. Dying patients in the United States and in India both claim to see this dark passage, brilliant light, and relatives previously deceased.

6. It should be noted, however, that religious background definitely influenced identification of any "being" that may have been encountered. No Christian saw a Hindu deity and no Hindu saw Jesus. The being does not seem to identify himself but is instead identified by the observer.

Dr. Charles Garfield, assistant professor of psychology at the University of California Medical Center, concludes from his observations that the whole quality of life-after-death visions is entirely different from drug-induced hallucinations or the kind of dissociated sensations that patients in a great deal of pain may experience. My own observations affirm this. Drug effects, alcoholic delirium tremens, carbon dioxide narcosis, and psychotic reactions deal more with objects in the present world and not with situations in the next world.

6

ASCENDING TO "HEAVEN"

Encounters in the next world are variously described as heavenly, pleasant, exhilarating, or beyond expression. Most of these descriptions, of course, represent interviews occurring away from the scene of resuscitation, usually a few days later. Many who have had these experiences are sure they are headed for a serene afterlife. For some, this could be true; others could have been given a false impression. Those who have had bad experiences do not remember them after being removed from the resuscitation scene, as evidenced by cases published thus far. We will discuss these bad episodes later, but now for the more pleasant ones.

Why should we publish all of the volunteered reports if some might not be representative? And what if they are not always "biblical"?

First, we must document the reports as they come until we are able to get a more accurate accounting by recording them at the actual times they occur. Secondly, we're not primarily concerned whether they compliment or coincide with any particular philosophical or religious belief. We first present them as they are. I will give you my observations, and how I feel these reports relate to Scripture. Your conclusions may be entirely different than mine.

VARIABLE EXPERIENCES

Pleasant experiences have considerable variability. Although the sequence of events is very much the same, some of the details may be omitted or altered from one experience to another. The following report concerns a lady in her twenties who saw herself dying, then leaving the scene, but never quite making it through the "tunnel":

I had lost a lot of blood. It was about an hour after I had delivered my only child. When they moved me from the stretcher to the bed to take me to surgery I could see the blood pouring through the separation between the bed and stretcher. It seemed to spurt each time my heart beat. It was an incredible loss of blood. I was sure my time was up.

They rushed me down to the operating room with blood splattering on the floor. When I arrived in the operating room I suddenly wasn't in my body. I don't remember getting out of it. But at least it didn't hurt. I was floating in the left-hand corner of the ceiling looking down at my doctor. I didn't like him. He was cursing and yelling at the nurses. I think he was panicked over my condition. Now I was sure I was going to die.

They were getting ready to give me an injection of medicine to put me to sleep but I was sure I would die before they could stop my bleeding. I saw the faces of my mother, husband, and baby boy who were all living. They would be sad at my death but I didn't feel despondent. In fact, it didn't seem to make much difference to me at all!

I wasn't unhappy and I couldn't understand why.

Next, I was hurdling down this dark tunnel at a high speed, not touching the sides. It made sort of a swishing sound. At the end of the tunnel was this yellow-white light. And then I said, "This must be what it feels like to die. I feel no pain at all." I was glad of that. But before I could get to the light and out of the tunnel, I found myself back in the recovery room that had four beds in it and I was in one of them.

I will never forget the peacefulness that I experienced. For some reason I was not afraid of this dying business, but I was glad to see my baby boy again!

Most cases have "indescribable" experiences: "I just can't find words to express what I want to say." Extremely pleasant feelings may be present despite coexisting discomfort from such things as head injuries, accidental crushing injuries, or gunshot wounds. At the moment of injury for instance, there may be a flash of pain and then all pain can sometimes vanish:

The pain left after the first bullet entered. I didn't feel the second or third. I had a feeling of floating in a dark space. In all this darkness I felt warmth and extreme comfort although my skin was extremely cold. I thought to myself, "I must be dead."

Astounding realizations and new concepts in life may occur, as they did in the following cases. Mrs. S. was struck by lightning while on a camping trip:

In the moment that I was hit, I knew exactly what had happened to me. My mind was crystal clear. I had never been so totally alive as in the act of dying. [Regrets of past actions together with things she wanted to do with her life filled her mind.]

At this point in the act of dying, I had what I call the answer to a question I had never verbalized to anyone or even faced: Is there really a God? I can't describe it, but the totality and reality of the living God exploded within my being and He filled every atom of my body with His glory. In the next moment, to my horror, I found that I wasn't going toward God. I was going away from Him. It was like seeing what might have been, but going away from it. In my panic, I started trying to communicate with the God I knew was there.

She begged for her life and offered it to God should He spare it. She recovered fully in three months.

"Floating" after separation from one's own body and the feeling of transition into a new dimension seem common in almost every case report:

I had pneumonia and was getting more toxic. My temperature was 107°. They told me later that I went into a coma for several days and they didn't expect me to live. I was packed in ice and given alcohol sponge baths. My family was told that nothing could be done and I would probably have severe brain damage if I survived.

During this coma, I found myself floating in a valley. There was a light in the distance on a mountain and as I approached the mountain I noticed beautiful orchids and flowers growing on its rocky slope. Among the boulders I saw my grandfather standing. He had been dead several years. I didn't talk to him but I knew I wanted to stay and I didn't want to come back.

I also saw a cross that was on the side of the mountain and a figure was hanging on that cross, still alive. I know it was Jesus. I had the sensation that this was both the beginning and the end of the world. After that, I suddenly found myself back in my body.

About three years ago, I had a similar experience when undergoing surgery for a degenerated hip joint. The joint degeneration seemed to be aggravated by cortisone treatment I had received. I was getting ready to undergo anesthesia when suddenly they thought I had died. I did not feel any separation of my spirit from my body nor did I recall any tunnel. I was just suddenly floating in the same valley that I had experienced previously. Only this time, both my grandfather and grandmother were there on the rocky mountain slope. My grandmother said, "You can't go with us. You have to go back." She was crying because I couldn't stay. I am not sure whether this was a judgment ground or what it represented. I do know that it changed my whole life. I enjoy life more now because I don't dread the future.

Separation from the body, like separation of vehicles in space, may occur in stages:

I had been in the hospital several days and my chest pain had already subsided. I was forty-six years old at the time and they could not find the cause of my trouble. I started packing to go home when I developed recurrence of the same severe chest pains. I was pushing the nurses' call button when I collapsed. Fortunately, the call button worked. Someone came into the room and called for help. Several other people soon came in and started working on me. One was pumping on my chest and another was getting oxygen.

About that time, I started drifting upward, leaving the discarded body behind and coming into the presence of a silvery, peaceful, brilliant light. I was not afraid and I wanted to stay. I then re-entered my body suddenly and without explanation. There was simultaneous recurrence of the same severe chest pain. As the pain subsided, once again I drifted up and out of my body, free of pain and then I thought "now I am really gone." And yet, I felt peaceful, wonderful. There was no fear of death. I had no meeting of any other people and no "tunnel" or flashback of previous life events that I had heard about in others.

Panoramic recall or instant replay of one's life, however, is a commonly reported observation; it is often similar to television flash-backs. It is not clear if this playback is a prelude to judgment or to anything else, but it is thought provoking.

I recall a particularly sad case, a man who died with an experience incompletely revealed. This patient had a common cold. Although I had told him that penicillin did not help colds or other viral illnesses, he was adamant that it always helped his own colds. After he reassured me that he had never had a reaction to penicillin, and upon his insistence, I gave him the penicillin injection.

Then it happened. He had what we call an anaphylactic reaction. Within five minutes of the injection, he crumpled to the floor unconscious, in deep shock, and without blood pressure. We started circulatory support with external heart massage until supportive drugs were obtained. An ambulance was summoned to transport him from the clinic to another hospital.

While awaiting the ambulance, he recovered his heartbeat and blood pressure, the latter with the help of a very powerful drug we were giving by intravenous drip method. This drug constricted the small arteries in his body, giving some support for blood pressure. He awoke and looked up into my face and said that he had just seen all of his life passing in review before him. Every important event seemed to be portrayed.

I was too busy to pay much attention at that time. For years I have been "too busy" to listen to my patients. Now it's too late in his case. He died with a cerebral hemorrhage as an indirect complication of the penicillin reaction. I actually broke down and cried.

Bliss, peace, and euphoria are readily described in the heavenly encounters as compared to the condemnations which we seldom hear reported.

As you may have already noticed, many of the "radiant" descriptions do not necessarily relate to "heavenly" experiences. One patient who was revived from a no-pulse, no-respiration, and dilated-pupil condition suddenly had a "new knowledge" of his relationship to his environment and to the world. The transition from life to death had been easy with no time for fear. He did not see his past life flash before him.

Moving at high speed through a net of great luminosity, he described going through what appeared to be a grid of luminous strands. After he stopped, this vibrant luminosity became blinding in intensity and drained him of energy. There was no pain and no unpleasant sensation. The grid had transformed him into a form beyond time and space. He was a new being. Personal fears, hopes, and wants were removed. He felt he was an indestructible spirit. As he was waiting for something momentous to occur, he suddenly returned to his body on the operating table.

Another patient described similar feelings of painless bliss when dying:

> I lost so much blood I was becoming unconscious. I felt my body separate. I was lying beside my own body. I looked over and watched the nurses and doctors working on my dead body. I myself felt very content and peaceful. I was free of pain and had a very happy feeling. I thought, if this was death it is beautiful. The thought of my family helped me to hang on to life, although I felt all

my troubles were gone at the time. I couldn't feel a thing except peace and ease and quietness.

The experience seems uniform: Actual death has no sting, no pain. The condition leading to death—the crushing auto accident, for instance—may be quite painful, but death itself is like a simple faint, a missed heartbeat, like going to sleep. These people with pleasant experiences are not afraid to die again.

ANGEL OF LIGHT

In a few cases, whether pleasant or unpleasant, the person does not recall actually leaving the body or experiencing transportation through a tunnel or any other passage. However, many of them recall meeting a heavenly being (or a grotesque being) or some form of a "take-away" figure. Some will identify the take-away figure as Jesus or an "angel of light" or some "holy being." I have not heard of anyone claiming to have seen the devil. It is interesting that whatever "being" they encounter has not, as a rule, identified himself. Usually the person having the experience makes the identification. Thus, the Hindus, Muslims, or Buddists may say that they see their deities while the Christians identify him as Christ. The following is an example of the latter:

Suddenly I felt relief from my terrible chest pains. Now I felt exhilaration. I can't fully express it. I was floating into an area that looked like heaven. It was wonderfully bright with buildings and streets of gold and I saw a figure with long hair in a brilliant white robe. A light radiated all about him. I didn't talk to him. I am sure that it was Jesus. As he took hold of my hand, the next thing I remember was a jerking on my body. You were shaking me and then the pain came back. But I

68

was back on earth again! I will never forget that moment of happiness. I want to recapture that moment again. I am not afraid of death. I really am not! I look forward to seeing Jesus again.

Other encounters with an "angel of light" are similar to this case:

I knew I was dying. They had just gotten me to the hospital and then I felt this pain in my head and I saw a great light and everything was whizzing around and around. Then I felt free and at peace and just an uncanny sense of well being. I looked down on the medical people working over me and it didn't bother me a bit. I wondered why.

Then I was suddenly enveloped in this black cloud and went through this tunnel. I emerged from the other end in a white light which had a soft glow. There was my brother who had died three years previously. I attempted to go through a doorway, but my brother was blocking my view and wouldn't let me see what was behind him.

Then I saw what was behind him. It was a bright angel. An angel of light. I felt encompassed by this force of love from this angel that was searching and probing my deepest thoughts. I was being searched and then I seemed to be allowed to sense the presence of spirits of some other loved ones who had died previously. Then my whole body jumped upward from the electric jolt they gave me, and I knew I was back on earth again.

Since I have recovered from this encounter with death, I am no longer afraid of death. I have already been there. I know what it is like.

This experience of meeting a "loving" or "searching" being of light in a beautiful environment is commonly reported. Confessed atheists have also told me of similar experiences, which, they say, proves there is no hell and that God, if He exists, loves everyone and therefore would punish no one.

In each account, however, the person is returned to his body before any decision is reached or any disposition is rendered. This initial encounter could conceivably represent merely a sorting ground. It could also represent a deceivingly pleasant situation to imply security and sanctuary and to prevent a desire or need for changed lives. This could be a satanic deception according to Charles Ryrie, Billy Graham, Stephen Board and other Christian spokesmen who quote 2 Corinthians 11:14. The following case involved a non-Christian patient:

> It was the third night I was in the coronary unit with a heart attack and I was awakened by the nurses and one of the men in white and they had a shot ready for me and I asked "what's the trouble?" One of the nurses said my monitor had stopped completely. I remember I asked them not to call any of my relatives as it was nearing the second-shift changing time and it was late. I held up my hand for the man to give the shot through the I.V. tube that was running in my arm.
>
> All at once I started ascending upward rapidly through this huge tunnel, round and round, not hitting the sides at all. I was saying to myself, "I wonder why I don't hit the sides of this?" Then I was stopped by this brilliantly lighted person. He knew my thoughts and reviewed my life. He told me to go back—that my time would come later. I felt welcome. I don't remember getting back in my body, but I remember them waking me up and telling me my heart had stopped and they had just started it up again.
>
> I was reluctant to tell my family because I didn't want to upset them about this strange experience.

Sometimes this light seems to illuminate the whole environment. It is usually described as a dazzling, though not blinding, light. Some describe a "being" in the light and others do not. In either event they seem to sense a thought-communication that this light affords with the whole environment. Those strong in their faith have no doubt that the light represents Jesus Christ. Some say that He identified Himself precisely.

The reference to light is mentioned in numerous instances in the Bible. Jesus, for instance, said,

> My light will shine out for you just a little while longer. Walk in it while you can, and go where you want to go before the darkness falls, for then it will be too late for you to find your way. Make use of the Light while there is still time; then you will become light bearers (John 12:35,36, TLB).

Light is also mentioned often in the Old Testament:

> The people who walk in darkness shall see a great Light—a Light that will shine on all those who live in the land of the shadow of death. For Israel will again be great, filled with joy like that of reapers when the harvest time has come . . . (Isa. 9:2, TLB).

In fact, I counted fifty-two entries in a biblical concordance under the heading "light." One is of particular interest. The conversion of Paul involved a light "brighter than the sun," which blinded him for three days. His companions heard the voice and saw the light but surprisingly were not blinded. None today who has seen a bright light during his experience was blinded by it, in spite of its apparent brilliance. The light Paul saw

71

is described in both Acts 9 and 26. The latter chapter contains Paul's report:

> When one day about noon, sir, a light from heaven brighter than the sun shown down on me and my companions. We all fell down and I heard a voice speaking to me in Hebrew, "Saul, Saul, why are you persecuting me? You are only hurting yourself."
>
> "Who are you, sir?" I asked.
>
> And the Lord replied, "I am Jesus, the one you are persecuting. Now stand up! For I have appeared to you to anoint you as my servant and my witness. You are to tell the world about this experience and about the many other occasions when I shall appear to you" (TLB).

CHANGED LIVES

Profound effects upon the future of one's purposes and beliefs seem to result from life-after-death experiences. Lives are changed:

> I always thought about social status and wealth symbols as the most important things in life until life was suddenly taken from me. Now I know that none of these are important. Only the love you show others will endure or be remembered. The material things won't count. Our present life is nothing compared to what you'll see later. Now I'm not afraid to die again. Those that are afraid of dying must have a reason, or else they don't know what it's like.

During spiritual existence some people report that they have heightened senses of perception. They may, for instance, notice a sweet smell to the air or beautiful music in the background or a euphoric existence.

The day following a violent storm in our city a few

years ago, a crew of men from the electric power company were throwing a grounding chain over some downed electric lines. Someone had neglected to turn the power off, and this chain happened to be entangled around the leg of one of the crewmen. He writhed along the ground, his body creating sparks as several thousand volts of current went through him, even burning the grass under him in spots. His fellow workers cut the chain loose and, after confirming no heartbeat nor breathing, began resuscitation. They had received emergency training from the utility company.

When I saw him in the hospital emergency room, he was still alive although unconscious. His pupils were normal, but several disturbances in heart rhythm required correction. A graft by our plastic surgeons was required to replace a large area of skin that had been destroyed by electrical burns of the ankle.

When he awoke the next day, he remembered hearing beautiful music and feeling an aura of quiet and peaceful existence long before becoming conscious. The odd thing was, he could still hear the music after he awoke. It intrigued him enough to ask a visitor to find out where the music was coming from. But the visitor could hear no music!

There were several other details that he could not recall, but this experience profoundly affected his whole life. Why music should have such an impact, I do not understand; however, since this experience he has been giving talks to almost any group or individual who will listen.

ENCOUNTERS BEYOND THE BARRIER

Entrance into hell (or what appears to be hell) may occur in a direct fashion, frequently by-passing most of the usual sequential order of events. In a similar manner, persons may report a direct entrance into heaven (or what appears to be heaven), although they seem more likely to first travel through some type of sorting ground or over some type of barrier. The sorting ground is usually a meeting area (true in both good and bad experiences) and the barrier is usually a fence or a wall or some similar obstacle.

A middle-aged, overweight male who had multiple deaths and multiple experiences before his final death, reported that some of these episodes had taken him to heavenly places. His high blood pressure caused repeated heart attacks, which in turn caused repeated episodes of fibrillation and sudden clinical death. Usually a convulsion would occur and then total loss of consciousness. All breathing would cease in two or three minutes if nothing was done, and each time electrical shock and resuscitation would bring him back. If any of these heart arrests had occurred at home, of course, permanent death would have resulted. As it was, these episodes of reversible death recurred every few days, and he would report an out-of-the-body experience each time. Only two of the experiences will be reported. The first, to illustrate a remarkable on-the-scene recall, and the second, to suggest a transition into a "heavenly" realm:

> I turned over to answer the phone and began to have another very severe pain in my chest. I pushed the button to summon the nurse and they came in and started working on me. They put medicine in the bottle hanging up on a stand beside the bed and running into my arm. I was miserable lying there. It felt like an elephant's foot standing in the middle of my chest. I was sweating and about to vomit when I noticed that I was losing consciousness. Everything was turning black. My heart stopped beating! I heard the nurses shouting "Code 99, Code 99!" One of them dialed the phone to the hospital loud speaker.

As they were doing this I could feel myself leaving by body from the headward portion, detaching and floating in the air without any sensation of falling. Then I was lightly standing on my feet watching the nurses push down on my chest. Two more nurses came in and one was wearing a rose on her uniform. Two more nurses came in and one orderly and then I noticed that they had gotten my doctor back from his visits in the hospital. He had seen me earlier. When he came into the room, I wondered why he was here. I felt fine!

Then my doctor took off his coat to relieve the nurse pushing on my chest. I noticed he had on a blue-striped tie. The room started getting dark and I had the sensation of moving rapidly down a dark corridor. All of a sudden I felt this horrible shocking in my chest. My body moved, my back arched and I felt this terrific burning in my chest like somebody had hit me. Then I woke up finding myself back in my bed. Only two nurses and an orderly were left. The others had gone.

The specific things this patient saw, including the number of people, what they did, and what they were wearing were subsequently verified. Reconstruction of the time sequence indicated that he was without heartbeat or consciousness during this entire interval of recall.

In contrast to most people who have been retrieved from death, this patient had an after-death experience each time he was resuscitated. Each experience was different. Each one was pleasant. This is one of the heavenly descriptions:

Again, that terrible pain returned in my chest. I knew it meant trouble. Maybe a faint. It had before. And I had been sleeping so nicely! I took my usual "dynamite" tablet under my tongue and yelled for the nurse. I pushed on the lights. The nurse came in quickly. The pain was worse. Then all of a sudden the room turned black again. I didn't feel any more pain.

The next thing I knew I was floating at the far end of the room near the ceiling, looking down on my body from the footward direction. I remember because I was saying to myself, "I didn't know I had such big feet. Could that really be me? There they are working on me again! I must have died!" I saw them wheeling in the EKG machine and close behind that was that shock machine. There seemed to be tubes all over the place, one of them going to my nose that must have been from the oxygen tank and another one in my arm. Meanwhile, I was floating up there with no way of falling. Then I heard them say, "I am not sure that he'll come back this time!"

That's all I remember in the room, and then I was going swiftly through a black tube, not touching the sides but soon I was glad to see light again but this time that wall didn't stop me. I actually flew right on over it. I was flying through space at a rapid rate.

There was a river below me, and it was becoming dawn. Everything was getting brighter. I noticed that I was crossing over a beautiful city below, as I followed the river like a soaring bird. The streets seemed to be made of shining gold and were wonderfully beautiful. I can't describe it. I descended onto one of the streets and people were all around me—happy people who were glad to see me! They seemed to be in shining clothes with a sort of glow. Nobody was in a hurry. Some other people were coming toward me. I think they were my parents. But just then I woke up, back in the hospital room. I was back in my body. This time I really wished they hadn't brought me back. I have been getting tired of going through all of this. Just let me stay.

This patient always had good experiences, none bad. He said he was a Christian, and he had already seen where he was going. He did not want to be brought back any more. He had had enough of shortness of breath and chest pains. Between episodes he tried to tell everyone who would listen about his experiences and about the next life—whether hospital staff or visitors. Then he got his wish. He didn't respond after the next episode.

Experiences of traversing barriers is not unusual in the Bible. Today there are cases that are reminiscent of descriptions of Stephen's, Paul's, and John's heavenly visions. One minister reports the following case:

> I was called in the middle of the night by the hospital nurse who informed me that Mrs. D., one of the parishioners at my little church, was dying. She asked me if I wanted to be present at her bedside. I dressed hastily and went to the hospital as quickly as I could. When I stepped off the elevator, the nurse told me, "I am sorry I called you out of bed. Mrs. D. is dead." She then took me into the room where Mrs. D., a little frail, silverhaired lady, had died from a terminal cancer. I was told that all vital signs had ceased. I prayed, simply talking out loud to God, saying that Mrs. D. had insisted on my coming for a purpose and I asked the Lord to let that purpose come to pass if it be His will.
>
> I then saw Mrs. D.'s eyelids fluttering and then some rustling occurred and then commotion in the room. Mrs. D. opened her eyes wide and stared straight at me. She spoke in a whisper, "I thank you, Pastor Grogan, for your prayer. I was just talking with Jesus and He was telling me to come back and do something for Him. I also saw Jim [her husband who had died a short time before]." She turned on her side and drew her knees up almost to her chin, breathing softly and slept.

As I walked down the corridor to the elevator, I heard the sounds of running feet. The nurse who had witnessed it all from the beginning overtook me and said, "I'm afraid! What did you do? That woman was dead and she came back to life! I have been nursing for many years and I never saw that happen before. I've always been an atheist."

Mrs. D., after she had recovered, had many conversations in which she described to others what she saw during her death: Jesus in His shining brightness and her departed husband Jim. She wanted to stay in heaven but Jesus had ordered her back to talk to others.

Then one day she called me to her home to tell me that she was going again to the hospital that very day—this time to go to heaven and stay. "Do not pray for me to live this time."

Another illustrative case is a patient who visited a heavenly city through angelic transportation:

My first pacemaker was inserted in March and it wasn't working well. I was in the hospital to get a new pacemaker put in. I asked my wife and brother-in-law to get the nurse. Something was going wrong with my heartbeat. I could feel it. Then I remember someone shouting "Code 99, Code 99." But I wasn't in the room after that. A nurse, it seemed, had grasped me from behind, encircling my waist with her arms, and took me out of there. We started flying out of the city, going faster and faster. The first time I knew it was not a nurse was when I looked down toward my feet and saw the tips of some white wings moving behind me. I am sure now it was an angel!

After soaring for a while, she (the angel) sat me down on a street in a fabulous city of buildings made of glittering gold and silver and beautiful trees. A beautiful light was everywhere—glowing but not bright enough to make me squint my eyes.

On this street I met my mother, my father and my brother, all of whom had died previously.

"Here comes Paul" I heard my mother say. As I walked to greet them, however, this same angel picked me up by the waist again and took me off into the sky. I didn't know why they wouldn't let me stay.

In the distance we were approaching the skyline. I could recognize the buildings. I saw the hospital where I had been sent as a patient. The angel descended and put me back in the very room where I had been located and I looked up and saw the faces of the doctors working on me. I was back in the body. I will never forget the experience. I don't think anyone could be an atheist if he had an experience like mine.

I was able to tape-record the following report made by a seventy-year-old accountant soon after he recovered his faculties. Most of his descriptions of heaven, although not completely reported here, closely resemble those given in the last two chapters of the Bible. In rare cases similar descriptions have been given by some who had never previously known the biblical descriptions of the New Jerusalem:

They were rushing me from the emergency room to the intensive care unit because of my chest pain. They told me it was a heart attack. In the elevator, I felt my heart stop and I stopped breathing and I thought, "This is it."

The next thing I remember was looking down on my body in the intensive care unit. I don't know how I got there, but they were working on me. There was this young doctor in a white coat and two nurses and a black fellow in a white uniform and he was doing most of the work on me. This black fellow was shoving down on my chest and someone else was breathing for me and they were yelling to "get this and get that!"

I learned later that this black fellow was a male nurse on the ward. I had never seen him before. I even remember the black bow tie he was wearing.

Next thing I remember was going through this dark passage. I didn't touch any of the walls. I emerged out into an open field and was walking toward a big white wall which was very long. It had three steps leading up to a doorway in the wall. On a landing above the stairs sat a man clothed in a robe that was dazzling white and glowing. His face had a glowing radiance also. He was looking down into a big book, studying.

As I approached him I felt a great reverence and I asked him, "Are you Jesus?"

He said, "No, you will find Jesus and your loved ones beyond that door." After he looked in his book he said, "You may go on through."

And then I walked through the door, and saw on the other side this beautiful, brilliantly lit city, reflecting what seemed to be the sun's rays. It was all made of gold or some shiny metal with domes and steeples in beautiful array, and the streets were shining, not quite like marble but made of something I have never seen before. There were many people all dressed in glowing white robes with radiant faces. They looked beautiful. The air smelled so fresh. I have never smelled anything like it.

There was a background of music that was beautiful, heavenly music, and I saw two figures walking toward me and I immediately recognized them. They were my mother and father, both had died years ago. My mother was an amputee and yet that leg was now restored! She was walking on two legs!

I said to my mother, "You and father are beautiful."

And they said to me, "You have the same radiance and you are also beautiful."

As we walked along together to find Jesus, I noticed there was one building larger than all of the others. It looked like a football stadium with an open end to the building where a blinding light radiated from it. I tried to look up at the light but I couldn't. It was too brilliant. Many people seemed to be bowed in front of his building in adoration and prayer.

I said to my parents, "What is that?"

They said, "In there is God."

I will never forget it. I have never seen anything like it. We walked on as they were taking me to see Jesus and we passed many people. All of them were happy. I have never felt such a sense of well being.

As we approached the place where Jesus was located, I suddenly felt this tremendous surge of electricity through my body as if someone had hit me in the chest. My body arched upward as they were defibrillating my heart. I had been restored to my former life! But I was not too happy to come back. However, I knew I had been sent back to tell others about this experience. I plan to dedicate the rest of my life to telling anyone who will listen!

For me, the excitement of discovering cases of beyond-the-barrier experiences is exhilarating. There has been no question in the minds of these people that their experiences were real and of momentous importance, and they want others to know about them. They are willing to dedicate their lives to telling any who will listen.

Borderline cases of near-entry into what could be initial judgment are not uncommon. Meeting friends and relatives previously deceased seems to be a fairly common and pleasant experience. Determination of their type of existence in the spiritual world may conceivably lie beyond the obstacle many of them seem to encounter.

Only a few people seem to pass over the barrier and return to tell us about it. For instance, there is the case of a Betty Maltz who was in a coma for forty-four days following a ruptured appendix. During this time she could still hear everything spoken in the room. Though her physical senses seemed to have diminished, the spiritual senses seemed to have been sharpened.

While in the coma she had an experience of walking uphill in a vivid environment. There was no fatigue, only a feeling of ecstasy. An angel was walking with her, but she saw only his feet. They came to a gate in a large marble wall, and she was invited to go on in and join in singing the beautiful hymns that were being sung. She was given the choice, however, of going back or going on through the gate.

Then she remembers surprising everyone by pushing off the sheets that had already been pulled over her face.[1]

All of the cases I have presented indicate a separation of the spirit from the body as a very fundamental occurrence at death. Listen to the Scriptures as they indicate why our present bodies of flesh and blood cannot enter the kingdom of God:

> In the same way, our earthly bodies which die and decay are different from the bodies we shall have when we come back to life again, for they will never die. The bodies we have now embarrass us for they become sick and die; but they will be full of glory when we come back to life again. Yes, they are weak, dying bodies now, but when we live again they will be full of strength.

---

[1] Mrs. Carl Maltz, *The Texas Herald*, Austin, Sept. 1977, pp. 6–7.

They are just human bodies at death, but when they come back to life they will be superhuman bodies. For just as there are natural, human bodies, there are also supernatural, spiritual bodies. . . .

I tell you this my brothers, an earthly body made of flesh and blood cannot get into God's kingdom. These perishable bodies of ours are not the right kind to live forever. But I am telling you this strange and wonderful secret: we shall not all die, but we shall all be given new bodies! It will all happen in a moment, in the twinkling of an eye, when the last trumpet is blown. . . .

When this happens, then at last this scripture will come true—"Death is swallowed up in victory. Oh death, where then your victory? Where then your sting? For sin—the sting that causes death—will all be gone; and the law, which reveals our sins, will no longer be our judge. How we thank God for all of this! It is he who makes us victorious through Jesus Christ our Lord! (1 Cor. 15:42–57, TLB.)

7

DESCENDING TO "HELL"

At last we turn to those reports that thus far have received little publicity. There are those who, after returning from clinical death, describe themselves as having been in hell. Some of these include the few who apparently broke through the barrier or great divide separating the sorting grounds from what could be the place of judgment. Those who did not encounter the barrier seemed to leave the scene of death to enter a different type of sorting ground—one that was morose and dark, similar to a carnival's "spook house." In most cases, this place seems to be underground or within the earth in some way.

HELL

Thomas Welch, in his booklet *Oregon's Amazing Miracle*, describes a most unusual experience in which he saw a tremendous "lake of fire, the most awesome sight one could ever see this side of the final judgment."[1]

While working as an engineer's helper for the Bridal Veil Lumber Company thirty miles east of Portland, Oregon, Welch was required to walk across a trestle over a dam fifty-five feet above the water where the sawmill was located. He then gives this account:

> I went out on the trestle to straighten out some timbers which were crossed and not moving on a conveyor. Suddenly I fell off the trestle and tumbled down between the timbers and into the pond, which was ten feet deep. An engineer sitting in the cab of his locomotive unloading logs into the pond saw me fall. I landed on my head on the first beam thirty feet down, and then tumbled from one beam to another until I fell into the water and disappeared from his view.
>
> There were seventy men working in and around the mill at that time. The mill was shut down then and every available man was called to search for my body, according to the testimonies of these men. The search went on for forty-five minutes to one hour before I was finally found by M.J.H. Gunderson, who has written his own account of this to verify the facts of this testimony.
>
> I was dead as far as this world is concerned. But I was alive in another world. There was no lost time. I learned more in that hour out of the body than I could ever learn while in this body. All I could remember is falling over the edge of the trestle. The locomotive engineer watched me go all the way down into the water.
>
> The next thing I knew I was standing near a shoreline of a great ocean of fire. It happened to be what the Bible says it is in Revelation 21:8: ". . . the lake which burneth with fire and

---

[1] Thomas Welch, *Oregon's Amazing Miracle* (Dallas: Christ for the Nations, Inc., 1976) p. 8. (Used by author's permission.)

brimstone." This is the most awesome sight one could ever see this side of the final judgment.

I remember more clearly than any other thing that has ever happened to me in my lifetime every detail of every moment, what I saw and what happened during that hour I was gone from this world. I was standing some distance from this burning, turbulent, rolling mass of blue fire. As far as my eyes could see it was just the same. A lake of fire and brimstone. There was nobody in it. I was not in it. I saw other people whom I had known that had died when I was thirteen. Another was a boy I had gone to school with who had died from cancer of the jaw that had started with an infected tooth while he was just a young lad. He was two years older than I. We recognized each other, even though we did not speak. They, too, were looking and seemed to be perplexed and in deep thought, as though they could not believe what they saw. Their expressions were those of bewilderment and confusion.

The scene was so awesome that words simply fail. There is no way to describe it except to say we were eye witnesses now to the final judgment. There is no way to escape, no way out. You don't even try to look for one. This is the prison out of which no one can escape except by Divine intervention. I said to myself in an audible voice, "If I had known about this I would have done anything that was required of me to escape coming to a place like this." But I had not known.

As these thoughts were racing through my mind, I saw another man coming by in front of us. I knew immediately who He was. He had a strong, kind, compassionate face, composed and unafraid, Master of all He saw. It was Jesus Himself.

A great hope took hold of me and I knew the answer to my problem was this great and wonderful Person who was moving by me in this prison of lost, confused judgment-bound souls. I did not do anything to attract His attention. I said again to myself, "If He would only look my way and see me, He could rescue me from this place because He would know what to do." He passed on by and it seemed as though He would not look my way, but just before He passed out of sight He turned His head and looked directly at me. That is all it took. His look was enough.

In seconds I was back entering into my body again. It was like coming in through the door of a house. I could hear the Brockes (the people I was staying with) praying minutes before I could open my eyes or say anything. I could hear and I understood what was going on. Then suddenly life came into my body and I opened my eyes and spoke to them.

It's easy to talk about and describe something you have seen. I know there is a lake of fire because I have seen it. I know Jesus Christ is alive in eternity. I have seen Him. The Bible states in Revelation 1:9-11: "I, John . . . was in the spirit on the Lord's Day, and heard behind me a great voice, as of a trumpet, saying, I am Alpha and Omega, the first and the last, and, what thou seest, write in a book."

Among the many things John saw was the judgment, and he describes it in Revelation 20 as he saw it. In verse 10 he says: "And the devil that deceived them was cast into the *lake of fire*. . . ." Again in Revelation 21:8, John says he saw the *"lake which burneth with fire and brimstone."* This is the lake I saw, and I am certain of this one thing, that in the end of this age at the final judgment every corrupt thing in this universe will ultimately be cast into this lake and be forever destroyed.

I thank God for people who can pray. It was Mrs. Brocke I heard praying for me. She said,

"Oh God, don't take Tom; he is not saved." Presently I opened my eyes and said to them, "What happened?" I had not lost any time; I had been gone somewhere and now I was back. Soon after this an ambulance arrived and I was taken to the Good Samaritan Hospital in Portland.

I arrived there just before six o'clock in the evening, was taken into surgery and my scalp was sewn with many stitches. I was put in the intensive care ward. There was really not much the doctors could do. It was simply a matter of wait and see.

During these four days and nights, I seemed to be in constant communication with the Holy Spirit. I relived the events of my past life and the things I had seen, such as the lake of fire, Jesus coming to me there, seeing my uncle and the boy I had been in school with, and the coming back to life again. The presence of God's Spirit was with me continually, and many times I spoke out loud to the Lord. Then I began to ask God what He wanted in my life, what His will was for me. . . . Then some time around nine o'clock the call of God came. The voice of the Spirit can be very real. He said to me, "I want you to tell the world that you saw, and how you came back to life."[2]

Another instance involves a patient dying with a heart attack. She attended church every Sunday and considered herself an average Christian.

I remember getting short of breath and then I must have blacked out. Then I saw that I was getting out of my body. The next thing I remember was entering this gloomy room where I saw in one of the windows this huge giant with a grotesque face that was watching me. Running

---

[2] *Ibid*, pp. 7–10.

around the windowsill were little imps or elves that seemed to be with the giant. The giant beckoned me to come with him. I didn't want to go, but I had to. Outside was darkness but I could hear people moaning all around me. I could feel things moving about my feet. As we moved on through this tunnel or cave, things were getting worse. I remember I was crying. Then, for some reason the giant turned me loose and sent me back. I felt I was being spared. I don't know why.

Then I remember finding myself back in the hospital bed. The doctor asked me if I had been taking drugs. My description must have sounded like the DTs. I told him I didn't have either of these habits and that the story was true. It has changed my whole life.

The variations in the figure that takes them away or sends them back from the spirit world seems to vary considerably among the bad experiences whereas in the good ones this figure seems to be similar from case to case.

I had severe abdominal pains from an inflammatory condition in the pancreas. They were giving me medicine for my blood pressure which was falling and my consciousness was slipping. I remember them working on me. I was going through this long tunnel and I was wondering why my feet weren't touching the sides. I seemed to be floating and going very fast. It seemed to be underground. It may have been a cave, but the awfullest, eery sounds were going on. There was an odor of decay like a cancer patient would have. Everything now seemed to be in slow motion. I can't recall all of the things I saw, but some of the workers were only half human, mocking and talking to each other in a language I didn't understand. When you ask me if I saw anybody I knew or if I met a beam of light, I did not. But there was a large person in radiant white clothes that appeared when I called, "Jesus, save me!" He looked at me and I felt the message "live differently!" I don't remember leaving there or how I got back. There are a lot of other things that may have happened that I don't remember. Maybe I'm afraid to remember!

In a modern "Charles-Dickens" account of travel to different worlds, George Ritchie, M.D., describes his death from a lobar type of pneumonia in 1943 while at Camp Barkley, Texas, at the age of twenty. In his excellent book *Return From Tomorrow* he describes how he unaccountably returned to life in nine minutes but during that time experienced a lifetime of adventure, some of it good and some of it bad. He describes a journey with a glorious being of flooding light and power whom he identified as Christ and who took him through a series of "worlds." The world of the damned in this instance existed on a vast plain that seemed to be on the surface of the earth where depraved spirits were at constant warfare with one another. Locked in personal combat, they punched and gouged at one another. Sexual abuses and howls of frustration were everywhere, and loathsome thoughts of anyone were universal knowledge of all. They could not see Dr. Ritchie or the figure of Christ with him, and the figure showed nothing but compassion and unhappiness that these people had sealed their own doom.

Rev. Kenneth E. Hagin recounts experiences that changed his whole life in his pamphlet *My Testimony*. The experience caused him to enter the ministry to tell others, and he relates the following:

. . . On the twenty-first day of April, 1933, Saturday night, 7:30 o'clock, at McKinney, Texas, thirty-two miles north of Dallas, my heart stopped beating and the spiritual man that lives in my body departed from my body . . . I went down, down, down, until the lights of the earth faded away. . . . The further down I went the blacker it became, until it was all blackness. I could not have seen my hand if it had been one inch in front of my eyes. The further down I went, the more stifling it was and the hotter it was.

Finally, way down below me, I could see lights flickering on the walls of the caverns of the damned. They were caused by the fires of hell. The giant orb of flame, white crested, pulled me . . . drew me like a magnet draws metal unto itself. I did not want to go! I did not walk, but just as metal jumps to the magnet, my spirit was drawn to that place. I could not take my eyes off it. The heat beat me in the face. Many years have now gone by, and yet I can see it with my eyes just as I saw it then. It is just as fresh in my memory as though it happened last night. . . .

Upon reaching the bottom of the pit, I had become conscious of some kind of spirit-being by my side. I hadn't looked at him because I could not take my gaze off the fires of hell, but when I paused, that creature laid his hand on my arm half-way between my shoulder and my elbow to escort me in. At the same moment, a Voice spoke, away above the blackness, above the earth, above the heavens. It was the voice of God, though I did not see Him, and I do not know what He said, because He did not speak in English. He spoke some other tongue, and when He spoke, it reverberated throughout the region of the damned, shaking it like a leaf in the wind, causing that creature to loose his grip. I did not turn around, but there was a Power that pulled me, and I came back away from the fire, away from the heat, back in the shadows of the darkness. I began to ascend, until I came to the top of the pit and saw the light of the earth. I came back into that room just as real as at any other time. I entered in through the door, except my spirit needed no doors.

I slipped right back down into my body as a man slips into his trousers in the morning, the same way in which I went out, through my mouth. I began to talk to my grandmother. She said, "Son, I thought you were dead. I thought you were gone."

. . . I would that I had words to describe that place. People go through this life so self-complacent, and as though they will not have to face hell, but God's Word and my own personal experiences tell me differently. I know what it is to be unconscious, and it is black when you are unconscious, but I want to tell you that there is no blackness like the Outer Darkness.

Many other "hell" cases are accumulating rapidly but will not be mentioned here. One that I should mention, however, involves a regular church member who was surprised in death to find himself descending through a tunnel lined by fire in its lower half, opening into a huge, fiery world of horror. He saw some of his old friends from the "good old days" who exhibited blank stares of apathy, who were burdened with useless loads, and who were continually going nowhere but never stopping for fear of "the main drivers" who, he said, were beyond description. Complete darkness outskirted the milieu of pointless activity. He escaped permanent captivity when he was summoned by God to come out in some miraculous way that is not clear. He has since been following a compulsive urge to warn others of the dangers of complacency and the need to take a definite stand in their faith.

SUICIDE

Suicide is attempted by many people to "end it all." According to the cases I've seen or heard about through other doctors, it may only be the "beginning of it all." I don't know of any "good" out-of-the-body experiences that have resulted from suicide. However, only a few who have attempted suicide have had experiences they will talk about. Here is an account described by one of my colleagues:

A fourteen-year-old girl became despondent over a report card from school. Communication with her parents usually centered upon her deficits, and recently upon her inadequacy to measure up to the grades of her sister who was a couple of years older and seemed to be accomplished in nearly everything. Even "looks" were compared. She never seemed to receive any praise, and now she had to confront her parents with her report card. She went up to her room, and thinking of the best way to solve the problem, she took a bottle of aspirin from the bathroom. It probably had eighty tablets in it, and she had to take a lot of water to get them down. Her parents found her a couple of hours later in a coma. She had vomited over her own face and onto the pillow. Fortunately, many of the aspirin had apparently not been absorbed and she recovered a couple of hours later in the hospital emergency room after we used a stomach pump and bicarbonate of soda to neutralize acidosis which caused a peculiar, heavy breathing, a characteristic of aspirin coma. (She was fortunate it was aspirin she took and not Tylenol, because the latter causes less vomiting and results in delayed damage to the liver that is frequently fatal.)

During one of the vomiting episodes she inhaled some of the vomitus, developed spasm of the vocal cords, stopped breathing and then had a cardiac arrest. She recovered immediately with external heart massage and placement of a breathing tube down her throat into her windpipe. Her recollections during the recovery were poor, but at the time she kept saying, "Mama, help me! Make them let go of me! They're trying to hurt me!" The doctors tried to apologize for hurting her, but she said it wasn't the doctors, but "Them, those demons in hell . . . they wouldn't let go of me . . . they wanted me. . . . I couldn't get back. . . . It was just awful!"

She slept for another day, and her mother hugged her most of that time. After the various tubes were removed, I asked her to recall what had happened. She remembered taking the aspirin, but absolutely nothing else! Somewhere in her mind the events may still be suppressed. Perhaps they could be reached with pentathol interview hypnosis. Frankly, I'm reticent to approach this area—it reminds me of demonology, a subject I respect but leave to others.

She subsequently became a missionary several years later. No despondency. I am told that everywhere she goes she brings exuberance—a contagious feeling.

The prevalence of depression, the prelude to suicide, is appalling. Suicide is the eleventh most common cause of death in the United States, acounting for approximately 25,000 deaths annually or a little less than 1.5 percent of all deaths. In teen-agers, next to automobile accidents, it is the most common cause of death. For each case resulting in death, it is probable that several more have attempted suicide unsuccessfully. This prevalence of suicidal thoughts, like bad experiences after death, tend not to be reported, much less discussed. They seem to be considered skeletons in one's life—something to hide and socially degrading. And yet therapy for this hurt, this warped emotional life, centers around release and discussion.

Because of emotional illness, our pharmaceutical market for tranquilizer drugs and antidepressants has skyrocketed. Most people I see seem to be on something. Valium is now the best money-maker and most popular drug in the United States next to the aspirin products.

The following case involved a fifty-four-year-old housewife with recurrent despondency:

> Nobody loved me. My husband and children used me as a servant. I was always cleaning up after them, but they acted as if I didn't even exist.
>
> One night I was crying and nobody listened. I took some Valium and told them I didn't want to live anymore. They still didn't listen, so I took a whole bottle of them—fifty of them.
>
> And then it was too late. I knew I had really done it. I was going to die! It was a sin—but so was living!
>
> As I got drowsy, I remember going down this black hole, round and round. Then I saw a glowing red-hot spot getting bigger and bigger until I was able to stand up. It was all red and hot and on fire. The earth was like slimy mud that sank over my feet, and it was hard to move. The heat was awful and made it hard to breathe. I cried "Oh, Lord give me another chance." I prayed and prayed. How I got back, I'll never know.
>
> They said I was unconscious for two days and that they pumped my stomach. They said my experience in hell must have been a drug trip. But they don't really know. I've taken Valium many times before, but never had an experience with it.

Another despondent lady, the mother of a twenty-four-year-old daughter who had committed suicide over a negligent boy friend, in turn tried to take her own life with an overdose of Amytal, a barbiturate, as soon as the daughter's funeral was over. She hoped to join her daughter. Instead of seeing her daughter, she found herself in what appeared to be hell, being jostled up and down on a blanket held between two satanic beings.

The scene occurred in a huge foreboding cave. The beings had tails and slanted eyes, she says, and looked horrible. After resuscitation and stomach washings she recovered and was told that her experience was probably due to drugs. She is still convinced it was not. She has received a new purpose and insight by the experience and is now organizing clubs for the emotional support of family survivors of suicide victims.

What are the practical consequences of suicide? Does suicide accomplish what the one attempting it intended? Is suicide indeed painless? Recently, a prominent, retired, closely devoted, childless couple looked to suicide as a cure-all. The woman had become confined to a hospital by a chronic lung disease, which had resulted in extreme oxygen dependency and mental derangement.

When her husband was told of the permanency of her problems, he decided to take her home for a few days to see if her despondency and confusion might improve with familiar surroundings. He said he wanted "to take care of her at home." He did.

Apparently unwilling to see his wife suffer with continual despair and discomfort, he shot her several times through the head. After calling a friend to tell him the circumstances, he then shot himself through the head. Unfortunately, he died. She lived. The point is, his attempt to improve a bad situation failed because his solution was wrong.

After this incident I realized I had been treating the wrong patient! I had missed the diagnosis of despondency and hopeless frustration in the husband. Instead, I had been paying my full attention to the patient who was occupying the bed. God's help wasn't even asked, much less considered. In reflection, I noticed this has always been one of my problems. In emergencies I ask for help automatically; in the more prolonged moments of despondency, I look for my own solutions.

LIGHT THAT IS DARKNESS

Perhaps we should mention again the controversy over the significance of the "beam of light" that has been encountered by many who have had after-death experiences. The light appeared in the "good" experiences and seemed to represent acceptance for all people. There was a sense of universal forgiveness, according to some—a general feeling of happiness and ecstasy, of indescribable peace and bliss. *In Life After Life*, Dr. Moody mentioned that he could not find a single reference to a heaven or a hell. There seemed to be no judgment when any sinful deeds of the individual were made manifest. There was no response of anger from the being of light but only "understanding."

Stephen Board takes issue with this observation. In his article "Light at the End of the Tunnel" he expresses his belief that the benevolent beam of light described by Moody reveals an air of moral tolerance and the philosophy "I'm okay, you're okay." To demonstrate that all cases do not involve an angel of light, Board reports an encounter with an "angel of death," as recorded by Dr. Phillip Swihart, clinical psychologist and director of Midwestern Colorado Mental Health Center, Montrose, Colorado:

> It was a Friday night, early in January 1967, when I was attacked, beaten, and kicked nearly to death. At the hospital the doctor decided to observe me the rest of the night and do exploratory surgery in the abdominal area in the morning. . . . While in the operating room awaiting surgery, I felt the presence of some thing or some power and I thought, "this is it." Next, blackness. Time became of no more importance.
>
> I had no idea how long I was without any

sensation in that darkness. Then it was light. I awoke and I knew it was real. In front of me, I watched my whole life pass by. Every thought, word and every movement I had made in my life since the time I knew that Jesus was real. I was very young when I took Christ as my Savior. I saw things I had done which I had forgotten but remembered as I watched them pass before me. This experience was, to say the least, unbelievable. Every detail, right up to the present time. It all took place in what seemed just a fraction of a second, and yet it was all very vivid.

All the time I was watching my life go by, I felt the presence of some sort of power, but I didn't see it. Next, I was drawn into total darkness. Then I stopped. It felt like a big hollow room. It seemed to be a very large space, and totally dark. I could see nothing, but felt the presence of this power.

I asked the power who I and who he or it was. Communication was not by talking but through a flow of energy. He answered that he was the Angel of Death. I believed him. The Angel went on to say that my life was not as it should be, that he could take me on but that I would be given a second chance, and that I was to go back. He promised me I would not die in 1967.

The next thing I remember I was in the recovery room, back in my body. I was so taken in by this experience that I did not notice what kind of body I had, nor how much time had elapsed, it was so real—I believed it.

Later in 1967, a car ran over my neck and shoulders. Still later in that year, I was in a car wreck in which both cars were totaled and in both accidents I came out almost completely unhurt. In neither accident was I at fault.

I did not tell many people about my experience; I did not want to be considered crazy. But the encounter was very real to me, and I still believe I was with the Angel of Death.[3]

Many theologians also take issue with the concept of universal forgiveness that is offered by the "angel of light" purportedly encountered by many patients having "good" experiences, whether their lives have been resplendent or not, whether they are believers or not. Seldom appearing in a bad light, Satan is capable of appearing as an angel himself (see 2 Cor. 11:14, 15).

Billy Graham reminds us there is a life after death for all people. However, those that have never accepted Christ as Lord and Savior "will go away into eternal punishment, but the righteous into eternal life" (Matt. 25:46). Since all will not be saved, some theologians remind us that Satan does not always appear evil but is a master of disguise, capable of the most clever deception. He can transform himself into an angel of light to convince the unsaved they are already saved or to neutralize the necessity of the Christian gospel.[4]

MULTIPLE EXPERIENCES

A few of the patients I have interviewed report multiple experiences from multiple deaths. At first these experiences may be bad and then good; so far, never in the reverse order. Some of them are similar to the first case I described—the man who said he was in hell and who then called for divine deliverance and who subsequently had pleasant experiences.

---

[3] Stephen Board, "Light at the End of the Tunnel," *Eternity*, July 1977, pp. 13–17. Reprinted by permission of *Eternity* Magazine, © 1977, Evangelical Ministries, 1716 Spruce St, Philadelphia, PA 19103.
[4] Eric Wiggins, "A Glimpse of Eternity," *Moody Monthly*, Oct. 1977. See also, Charles C. Ryrie, "To Be Absent From the Body," *Kindred Spirit*, Summer 1977, pp. 4–7.

I recall a similar case, one I find difficult to explain. This involved a staunch Christian, the founder of a Sunday school, and a lifelong supporter of the church. He experienced three different episodes of heart attack, three different episodes of fibrillation, three different episodes of successful resuscitation, and three different after-death experiences. The first episode was terrifying; the next two were quite pleasing and even euphoric.

> I don't remember the circumstances prior to the first time I passed out. They told me I had died, and when I woke up I found two red areas the size of small saucers, one over my left chest and one over the upper breastbone area. They said this was where the shock paddles were applied. I don't remember that either. I do remember you asking me, as soon as I woke up, what had happened. The only thing I remember was passing out into blackness and then I saw these red snakes crawling all over me. I couldn't get away from them. I would throw one of them off and then another one would get on me. It was horrible! Finally, I was dragged down to the ground by something and then other crawling things started getting on me. Some looked like red jelly. I screamed and cried out, but no one paid any attention to me. I had the impression there were many other people in the same fix all around me. It sounded like human voices and some of them were screaming. It was reddish black in there and hazy and hard to see, but I never did see any flames. There wasn't any devil, just these crawling things. Although my chest hurt real bad, I remember how glad I was to wake up and get out of that place. I was sure glad to see my family. I never want to go back there. I am convinced it was the entrance to hell.

Without any apparent reason, unless some secret transformation or dedication occurred of which I am

unaware, this patient's subsequent two experiences during other deaths were beautiful. He tried to describe one
of them as follows:

> I remember the nurse had come into the
> room to start oxygen through a tube in my nose
> because of the severe chest pains that were recur-
> ring. She said she was going to leave for a minute
> to get a shot for my pain. I remember as she was
> saying that that I must have fainted because she
> yelled out the door to the other nurse who was
> on duty at the diagnostic center that night,
> "Come in here quick! Mr. Ledford has had a
> heart arrest!" That's all I remember. Everything
> was black, and then I remember seeing them
> working on me and it seemed so strange because
> I felt perfectly fine. I had to move to one side to
> see my face to make sure it was my body. Just
> then, about three or four more people came in.
> One of them was a boy in charge of oxygen, and
> the others seemed to be nurses from another unit.
> Then everything seemed to be dimming out and
> going black again. I was moving through this
> long corridor and after a while I noticed a small
> pinpoint light that looked like a bird and then
> this slowly became larger and larger until it
> looked like a white dove that was flying and it
> kept getting bigger and bigger and brighter and
> brighter, expanding until the whole area was lit
> with this brilliant, beautiful light. I have never
> seen anything like it before. I found myself on a
> rolling green meadow that was slightly uphill. I
> saw my brother and he was alive, and yet I re-
> member when he had died. He was so glad to see
> me. We put our arms around each other right
> there in the middle of the meadow. I had tears in
> my eyes and then we strolled arm in arm up the
> meadow. I remember that it was uphill a bit and
> then we came to a white fence that looked like a

split rail, but I couldn't get over it. Some force seemed to keep me from getting over that fence. I didn't see anybody on the other side and there didn't seem to be any reason why I couldn't get over that fence!

The next thing I remember I was feeling this thud on my chest; somebody was pounding on me and pushing on me. I thought my ribs were breaking and I woke up looking up into your face! I remember I didn't want to come back. It was beautiful beyond expression, what I had seen!

This was his second experience. He was able to recall vivid details of the wonderful existence, but he couldn't recall details of the painfully unpleasant first experience, nor could he volunteer an explanation for its occurrence to a professing Christian.

His third experience was also pleasant and easily recalled:

I was floating over this beautiful city, looking down. It was the prettiest city I have ever seen. People were there. All in white. The whole sky was so lit up, brighter than sunshine. I was about to drift down and walk around in this city when I found myself back in my body, feeling the most terrible shock again as they put the paddles to me to revive my heart. Except for my wife's sake, I wish you hadn't brought me back.

This patient finally got his wish. He died a fourth time a few months later, from cancer of the large bowel. This condition was entirely unrelated to the repeated heart attacks, which I had been certain would be the ultimate cause of his death. I've often wondered what he's doing now.

8

DEALING WITH THE DYING

Contemplation of death, for the purpose of our discussion, involves a person who knows or is convinced he is dying, usually dying from a dreaded disease. As it happens, he is the most neglected of our patients and perhaps the most lonely. He may be full of questions, but no one will listen or offer answers.

Most terminally ill people intuitively know they are dying without being told. Thus, some marvelous theatrical performances take place in the hospital room as visitor and patient each pretends the other doesn't know, and with very guarded conversation each attempts to deceive the other. Dying patients need the close relationship and sympathy from someone who knows and can relate to him. The dying patient should no longer be the neglected patient. Physical death is a fact of life, but to allow spiritual death because of fear of discussing it would be a heartless folly.

Most of us avoid the thought of dying. The very subject is disruptive. We often treat those who are terminally ill as if they have a social disease. We shut them up in hospitals and deprive them of all the pleasures that once made their lives full and meaningful: children, friends, music, good food, home, love, and honest conversation. But soon it will be our turn to occupy that same bed, face that same calamity of life, and contemplate death.

Suppose you were suddenly told by your doctor you had an incurable disease and did not have long to live, what would be your reaction? Disbelief? Disallowance? Depression?

Of the vast literature dealing with death, extensive case reports of the dying patient have been internationally accumulated and analyzed by two psychologists, Dr. Karlis Osis and Dr. Erlendur Haraldsson, in their book *At the Hour of Death*.[1] Dr. Phillip Swihart has added other cases in his book *The Edge of Death*.[2] Dr. Elisabeth Kubler-Ross, a psychiatrist, deserves special recognition as a pioneer in the study of the dying patient and it is to her conclusions that we now turn.

THE FIVE-STAGE PROCESS

Having interviewed more than two hundred patients, Kubler-Ross outlines in her book *On Death and Dying* a pattern of five progressive stages in the emotions of the average patient who is awaiting death: *denial, anger, bargaining, depression*, and *acceptance*.[3]

1. *Denial*. Almost always the first emotional stage experienced by the dying patient is denial. To him, death is a catastrophic announcement of doom. The patient may withdraw into a solitary terror of his imminent nothingness. "This could not happen to me!" "The

---

[1] Drs. Karlis Osis and Erlendur Haraldsson, *At the Hour of Death* (New York: Avon Books, 1977).

[2] Dr. Phillip Swihart, *The Edge of Death* (Downers Grove, Ill.: Inter-Varsity Press, 1978).

[3] Elisabeth Kubler-Ross, *On Death and Dying* (New York: The Macmillan Co., 1969) *passim*.

diagnosis is wrong!" "The X rays were mixed up!" "There has been some error in diagnosis!" To support this denial, the patient may see many doctors.

Such denial serves as a buffer after the unexpected news. It allows the patient time to compose himself and perhaps to employ other less radical defenses. This does not mean, however, the patient will not later wish to talk about his impending death; rather, he may be willing and relieved to converse with someone who is really interested. On the other hand, some patients may be the first to realize they are dying, even before the doctor is aware of it. They may want to talk about it but are unable to find listeners. In fact, nobody seems to want to talk about death. Perhaps it is a distasteful subject, or perhaps it presents a threat to one's own existence.

A frightening change in America's cultural heritage seems to be occurring in regard to senior citizens. Two million Americans die each year, and since more than eighteen million Americans are now over sixty-five, about eighty percent of these deaths occur in nursing homes or hospitals instead of in private homes where the dying person can be with his family. Hence, the death event has been transferred from the home to the hospital and is being handled rather poorly by all concerned. We physicians have had no formal training for the emotional care of the aging patient or the dying patient—only the sick patient.

Furthermore, the hospital environment for the dying patient has become most efficient, and, therefore, almost completely depersonalized. In the usual intensive care ward, for instance, the family is allowed access for only five minutes each hour while the patient spends the remaining time in the care of strangers. The sicker he is, the more mechanical gadgetry is involved. The more ill he becomes, the more injections he is given, the less personal contact he feels, and the stranger the environment seems—and he dies friendless and alone.

As diseases of the young and middle-aged are prevented or cured, the number of living elderly grows. With the survival of the elderly, the frequency of malignancies and chronic diseases of aging are increasing. If present trends continue, economic problems will occur as the number of elderly becomes greater than the number of those physically able to support them. Even now, the tendency seems to be for the average family to divest itself from the care of their elderly dependents, transferring them instead to nursing homes or perhaps into the obscurity of some other human junkyard.

I remember one elderly patient who existed in a depressing atmosphere in a rather repugnant nursing home. A forgotten patient among other depraved souls, he was treated as a protoplasmic nonentity. One day he became acutely ill with pneumonia and was transferred to the nearest hospital where antibiotics, oxygen, and intravenous medications were to no avail. Although medical treatment was good, he died. He had received no treatment of the emotions and no care for the soul. He was friendless, frightened, forgotten, and alone. There was no opportunity for him to talk to anyone about finances, family, religion, or death. And no one asked him if he was prepared for life after death.

Dialogue of this sort, of course, should take place in privacy, at the convenience of the patient and only with his approval. The conversation should be terminated when he shows no interest in the subject or resumes his previous denial. These subjects should be broached before his illness renders his faculties and mind unapproachable. If the interviewer remains available, even if the patient does not feel like talking on the first or second encounter, he may soon develop a feeling of confidence that the interviewer cares and really wants to know him. The patient usually wants to share his loneliness and frequently becomes open and candid and allows a meaningful relationship to develop.

2. *Anger* is usually the second stage. This occurs after the patient has overcome the devasting blow of the initial news followed by the reaction "It can't be me." Denial is replaced by anger—by feelings of envy, rage, resentment, and the question "Why me?" or "How could a loving God do this?"

The stage of anger, in contrast to the stage of denial, is very difficult to manage. Patients may think or say things like this: "The doctors don't know anything. They don't even know how to take care of me." These patients are very demanding of the nurses and the aides, constantly wanting attention. Nothing suits them.

One of my heart patients, a sixty-eight-year-old lady, developed this angry, critical attitude. She became very irritable. To her the food was bad, the service was terrible, and turning to me during one visit, she said, "Even you are getting so that you never do anything right." Short-tempered, she was critical of everyone, particularly her husband. He finally left her. Her stage of anger and resentment persisted in spite of her loneliness. Although her impending death with heart disease has since been corrected, her bitterness has not. She seems mad at the world and mad at God.

3. *Bargaining*, sometimes the third stage, is a debatable issue among doctors who either agree or disagree with Kubler-Ross. The anger stage may be replaced by attempts at good behavior, hoping to please or bargain with God since anger didn't help. This stage seems to be brief.

I recall one patient who promised to dedicate his life to God and donate his money and time to the church if only God would spare him. He was spared, but he soon forgot his promise.

This bargaining stage reminds me of those sudden calamities where people who usually remember God only in cursing now call on Him fervently. Acutely injured patients either seem to call "mama" or "Jesus."

During the stage of bargaining, the patient eventually acknowledges God even if he never has before.

4. *Depression* is often the fourth stage. When the terminally ill patient can no longer deny his illness and predicament, his anger and rage are soon replaced by a sense of great loss. Although this sense of loss may be initiated by losing one's job, the effects of surgery, or the anxiety of leaving behind the good things of life, the most frightening loss he faces is that of himself. Loss of hope, when it occurs, represents the final decay of the person. Among Dr. Kubler-Ross's patients, both atheists and people of strong faith were able to accept death with more equanimity and less depression than those of lukewarm beliefs.

The depression stage has taken different forms in my own patients. I recall, for example, a cancer patient so depressed that he would not speak to anyone—nurses, family, or friends—except to nod his head yes or no. In addition to his terminal illness, his depression was compounded because he felt responsible for someone else's death. Later he discovered that the other person's death was actually caused by illness, and he was then able to cope with his own death. He became inquisitive about life after death and soon began talking freely with his family.

5. *Acceptance* is considered the fifth stage. After depression and the thoughts of the impending loss of fond friends and memories, he finally faces the end of his own life with a certain degree of acceptance and quiet expectation. However, there is still an attitude of withdrawal, an apathy. Finally there may develop a regard for the world as a worthless place, emphasizing the unpleasant things of this life.

Although the patient may accept his impending death, the family may refuse to accept it. The family members may avoid discussing with him the things about which he wants to know most: Is death painful?

Is there life after death? How do I prepare for it? How can I be sure?

CONTEMPLATION AND PREMONITIONS

Not many dying patients have died with the security of another life. For example, Leo Tolstoy in writing *The Death of Ivan Ilyich* gives a horrifying description of an expression that was fixed upon a dead man's face while he lay in his coffin. The expression represented the final stage in the tragedy of watching himself die.

Almost identical stages during contemplation of death were previously recorded by Tolstoy that were subsequently enumerated by Kubler-Ross. Tolstoy's Ivan fell from a ladder and injured his side. The wound eventually initiated an undiagnosed illness, which slowly and painfully led to his death. The reality of impending death had the effect of forcing Ivan Ilyich to examine his life.

He recalled some pleasurable moments of childhood and youth but remembered his adulthood as "ugly and senseless." Contemplating death, he saw that his life seemed "inversely proportioned to the square of the distance from death." Three days of horrible screaming followed as he resisted death. Finally, he accepted his life as worthless and meaningless. Then there was peace. Instead of fear, there was a type of joy taking place in a "saving" knowledge.

This transformation seems curious for there was no hint of an afterlife in the death of Ivan Ilyich. Life seemed to exist only for this world. The redeemed life of Ivan lasted for only a moment, since death was oblivion. Tolstoy apparently believed this was sufficient. Reality for Tolstoy was in the now, and this is also characteristic of Russian ideology today.

One particular patient I recall had a premonition of death and wanted to talk about it with his family. He seemed to sense that tomorrow would be too late. It was.

Perhaps we should listen more closely to premonitions of the dying patient. For some uncanny reason their premonitions are often accurate. We should also have less fear in talking more openly with the dying patient. If he wishes to talk about his illness, then we should accept the invitation and develop the conversation on the patient's terms and try to answer his questions.

It is interesting that in more than two hundred patients approached by Kubler-Ross, she mentions only three who refused to be interviewed. Other doctors also find that patients do indeed desire to talk about themselves, their condition, their prognosis, and even death itself.

WHAT I SAY

When a patient asks me about his chance of surviving a serious illness, I try never to remove all hope by emphasizing the certainty of death. I find it much more helpful to tell the patient truthfully that he has a serious disease (which I am frank to call by name) which could kill him; that he should prepare himself in case it is fatal, and that he should have things settled with God so that either way he can't lose. Pray for a miracle, but be prepared for anything.

As a Christian I also ask him if he's sure he knows where he will spend eternity. If he isn't sure, I ask him if he would like to arrange things so he can be sure. To my knowledge, *I have never seen a dying atheist.* I have talked to many ministers, however, who have indeed known dying patients who completely rejected "religion" of any kind, including Jesus Christ.

I have been observing how both the clergy and the doctors deal with the dying patient. It is interesting that neither of the professional groups seem at all eager to establish any meaningful relationships with the dying patient. My thesis keeps getting stronger—the dying patient is the *most neglected* of all patients, except for those with contagious illnesses. Both the minister and the physician seem to have been inadequately trained in either seminary or medical school to deal with those who are dying. Death may also be viewed as an unpleasant reminder of their own mortality.

Family members usually feel uncomfortable around the dying patient. Death remains a socially unacceptable disorder, something to be shunned, avoided, and denied. Confrontation is often postponed, hoping the threat will magically disappear.

Except during the stage of denial when no one wants to talk about death, the patient wants knowledge, preparation, and reassurance. If he does not have assurance, he wants it; if he already has it, he wants more. Although he may have rejected the Good News before, now he's quite interested. He may want to know how to rededicate his life. You are his doctor, or you are his friend, and you have an attentive audience.

The dying patient is more likely to listen to you and me than to a peacher. The patient recognizes us as members of "Sinners Anonymous," ones with whom he can identify since we are sinners just as he is. He is interested in our beliefs. If we can believe the Bible, then, he figures, maybe so can he.

On the other hand, many patients don't consider the pastor a sinner—no, he's a preacher, not a sinner. They may think, "How can he understand my problems?" If we,—you and I, people like the patient—believe that Jesus Christ is alive and well today, then the patient can believe this too! He wants to hear it from us! And yet this is the very person we have been avoiding!

We doctors, after writing orders on the patient's

chart and a brief examination of the patient, conveniently disappear to avoid the patient's questions concerning his chances of survival and what happens if he dies. Similarly, the minister may enter the room, open the Bible, read a verse or two, say a prayer, and then also conveniently disappear to avoid the unasked questions—which need answers now more than they ever did before.

If we rely on the average minister instead of ourselves to answer these questions, they may go unheeded. Suppose the clergy could especially train the lay people for this type of ministry, and the flock could learn to minister to the flock. This sinner-to-sinner, one-on-one approach might afford a high yield of effectiveness in reassuring the dying patient.

I remember a judge who developed a malignant lymphoma, a fatal disease that invades the blood-producing organs of the body. He knew the disease would act like a leukemia and would eventually result in death.

In discussing the details of his illness, he asked if his death would be painful. I told him no; I would be able to arrange medications in sufficient doses near the time of his death so he would be without pain. I assured him he would be unafraid, unaware, and unconcerned.

At times the conversation turned to other matters. As with other dying patients, this judge displayed an eagerness to hear about biblical truths that he had previously discarded or conveniently disregarded. I was actually surprised when he said he wanted assurance of salvation. He wanted to commit his life, whether he lived or died, to Jesus Christ. He asked me to pray with him. I told him I wasn't a minister, but he wasn't concerned. He was overjoyed. My prayer didn't sound too good to me, and I was amazed that I did it, because I was so new at all this myself.

He soon developed an attitude of expectation and

was no longer afraid to talk about his death. He was a tough old gentleman, a scholar, and a sportsman. He was also independent. But now he had turned to Christ. No minister seemed to have had much influence on him. But he was open to a layman's witness. God could use even someone like me.

Similarly, a newspaper man whom I had been treating previously for heart disease developed cancer of the pancreas, a digestive organ in the abdomen. This cancer was both inoperable and incurable, and the patient knew it. I saw him daily on rounds in the hospital, but didn't mention or discuss his impending death.

Then, one day he asked me privately if I believed in God. What an opening! He was asking me what I believed. He was a learned man, versed in philosophy, but still searching for the purpose of life and still ignorant of spiritual things. The discussion that followed was friendly, open, and comfortable for both of us. Discarded scriptural passages started to take on meaning—with insights *I* had never known before. He seemed to develop some sort of personal relationship with Jesus Christ. There wasn't enough literature to keep him occupied. A change in personality gradually occurred. Each day he became more considerate of the nurses, more loving to his family, and was always inquiring about the welfare of other people, never mentioning himself. "Did you have a nice day?" he would say. "Sit down and tell me about yourself." And it didn't matter who the person was.

And in this fashion, he died—counting on Christ and loving the devil out of others!

An article by Hadley Read recounts his love for his dying son. Philip was of college age and was dying with a spreading cancer. In this story the conspiracy of silence that usually surrounds the sick room was gradually replaced with honesty and candor in discussing his illness. The groping, the hesitance, the avoidance of

115

truth that usually plague the relatives and friends of the dying patient were finally dispelled. Gradually, there was a tendency to speak freely, to express compassion and love, to offer understanding, and to share companionship during the lonely vigil of death.

Mr. Read tells how his own hearing difficulty caused him to write notes to his son. He requested his son to share everything with him including his pain, his discomfort, and his fears. Mr. Read wanted to be near. By mutual consent they talked about death, about facing its reality, about where he would like to be buried, and about a special request Philip made: "Promise that you will not let them keep me alive just for the sake of keeping me alive. I do not want to live without a functioning mind. I only want to live if I am aware that I am alive—if I can enjoy being alive. That is very important to me."[4]

His father said he understood and agreed and would want the same thing. After Philip's death, his father composed some verses to express his love for his son:

> *Where did you go*
> *On your magic carpet*
> *When you closed your eyes*
> *And left so quietly in sleep?*
> *I think I know.*

What an opportunity is ours to "buy up" every opportunity to introduce the dying to Jesus Christ—and to be sure of Him *ourselves!* Woody Allen, the comedian, has dwelt on his morbid preoccupation with death. When an interviewer commented that Allen had already obtained immortality through his achievements,

---

[4] Hadley Read, "Conversations with a Dying Son," *Farm Journal Inc.,* Mid-Feb. 1976, pp. 38–41.

Woody's reply was: "Who cares about achieving immortality through achievements? I'm interested in achieving immortality through not dying."

Billy Graham, on the other hand, in his book entitled *Angels,* indicates that he actually looks forward with anticipation to death. He expects to be with Jesus Christ and to see Him face to face. He anticipates seeing family members and friends who have died previously. Some people are acutely afraid of death when they learn there is another life. But putting Christ first really does remove the fear of death.

Contemplation of death *while we are still in good health* affords us an excellent utilization of time and objectives during our short pilgrimage on earth. Our present life is not everlasting, and we stand as being accountable. Since there is no rationale for death without faith, it follows that faithless contemplation of death represents no more than destructive oblivion. But if these people are correct who tell us they have seen a life after death, then we have been betting our lives on the wrong thing. It is not safe just to die!

9

WHAT'S IT ALL ABOUT?

If life after death actually occurs, why then is judgment rarely mentioned in case reports? Perhaps the individual sojourns are too short, or maybe these people would not be permitted to return to life if permanent judgment were passed. Although the reports indicate the kind of afterlife each person involved faces, the ultimate destination is not always clear. In the case of the unpleasant occurrences, the true outcome implied by the experience will probably remain partially obscured by the very nature of the damning indictment, and we hope the subsequent redirection of one's life will replace condemnation with salvation.

If there is life after death, if there is a metamorphosis with an uninterrupted continuation of the spirit outliving the body, then we are talking about life without death.

This concept of spiritual immortality is abhorrent to some Protestant faiths that prefer to believe the spirit dies at the same time as the body, and both are subsequently revived at the day of resurrection. In answer to this, I can only report what these patients tell me. They are convinced they have had an opportunity to look first hand, and they are willing to dedicate their lives to telling others. I can find no reason to doubt their reports that life after death occurs *immediately* and that the body is dead when the spirit leaves it. In fact, Jesus Himself taught that a conscious existence continues after death, that there is a "good place" and "bad place" prior to final judgment, and, incidentally, that the dead are not allowed to talk with the living (see Luke 16).

But the main issue among Christians has already been agreed upon: that there is a Creator of life, and in another dimension man, whether good or bad, will live again. But not all people will agree. Not all believe in a Creator. And the reasons for this vary.

A COSMIC BOOM?

Is God real? Or is the universe really the result of the "Big Bang," an explosion of an original large mass of matter that created many smaller stars? And where did this original mass of matter come from? Or was there a Creator? And where did He come from? And did He also create life? Could there have been a Supreme Intelligence who directed and controlled the orderly unfolding of a universe that today continues to obey precise physical laws?

The late scholar Edwin Conklin, a professor of biology, compared the probability of life originating by accident to the probability of an unabridged dictionary being produced by an explosion in a printing shop. Yet many highly educated men say there is no God—just science. They forget, as we have already mentioned, that the god of science is forever changing and requiring updating and revision, while the God of the Bible remains the same yesterday, today, and forever. Perhaps some people try to hide themselves in atheism or agnosticism since belief in God would require accountability to Him. Other people are looking for God through a myopic vision, when they merely need to look up from themselves and see His creation that speaks of Him everywhere. Certainly the chaos of chance could not have evolved into the present cosmos of order.

Who is God to you personally? Your answer to whether or not God exists is important. If you consider it seriously it is the most important answer in life. It not only determines your future but also the way you live in the present. Therefore, one of the most difficult concepts I have ever personally faced is represented in the first four words of the Bible: "In the beginning God. . . ." Once through faith I moved over this hurdle, everything else fell into place. I still cannot comprehend the vastness of God's power or the purity of His holiness. How can one so terrible in justice at the same time be so loving and merciful? His righteousness terrifies me. Yet His love overwhelms me and breaks my pride. My comprehension of Him is limited by my mortal mind, which cannot begin to contain Him or define Him. And yet I know Him personally through Jesus Christ. He is my heavenly Father.

There is a story of a man who gave a garden party one evening. The patio was decorated with brightly burning Japanese lanterns. One of the guests, who was known for his agnosticism, asked who had hung the lanterns. The host, looking up into the beautiful night sky, noticed the stars burning brightly and asked his guest how he thought the stars got there. After a little thought he said, "I don't know—I guess they just got hung up there by themselves." The host replied, "That's exactly how my Japanese lanterns got there—by themselves."

THAT ENDLESS SEARCH

In almost all the world's religions men seek after God. By some inborn sense, man seeks God, or at least purpose in life. Only in Christianity do we have God seeking man, revealing Himself through the prophets in the Old Testament and revealing Himself through his Son in the New Testament. Still, God remains incomprehensible. There is no way to conceive of His origin or to know His habitation. There is no beginning or end. Yet through faith, He can become nearer than hands and feet. The mystery of the Creator is summarized by Moses in Psalm 90:2: "Before the mountains were born, or Thou didst give birth to the earth and the world, Even from everlasting to everlasting, Thou art God."

God's covenants with man remain unbroken, while man continues to break his convenants with God. To take God's name in vain, for example, has become socially acceptable. Few are disturbed when someone "God damns" something. In fact, nonbelievers seem to use Jesus's name more than Christians. Yet when those same individuals face calamities, more often than not they call on Jesus for help.

Once many years ago I remember drinking one too many at a cocktail party. I got terribly dizzy, and when I tried to go to sleep it seemed as if the bed wouldn't stay still. I started vomiting. I began to pray out loud, "God get me over this and I'll never do it again." I drank ginger ale and Cokes at parties for some time after that. But it didn't take me long to forget my promise; and after the first cocktail, it didn't take me long to forget everything else I had ever promised Him. One mistake became an excuse for another. The covenant was broken.

Just as I have done, many people in times of emergencies call on God to help them. Why should He? Why should He recognize us if we haven't recognized Him? Why should He honor our requests if we don't honor His?

One day I was flying home from Nashville on an instrument flight plan in my faithful old Aztec. I was happily darting in and out of clouds when I inadvertently entered a storm cell. Daylight turned into pitch-black darkness. Rain suddenly appeared from nowhere, beating on the windshield in torrents of such strength that mists of water penetrated through the seams of the windshield. My passengers started bouncing around in spite of their fastened seat belts. My head was hitting the ceiling. This time I was *really* scared.

With a shaky voice I called the nearest control center to give me a radar vector heading to get out of the storm. They said they couldn't see that particular storm cell on their radar scope. The center had been tracking me on radar but had not seen the storm. Bully for them, I thought, but that didn't do *me* any good. I told them maybe they couldn't see this thing, but it sure wasn't my imagination. "Help me out of it!" I pleaded.

By that time hail had begun pelting the plane and lightning had started flashing over on my right. It seemed we had been in this fix for an hour, but now I'm sure it was only a few minutes. Then, just as suddenly as it had happened, black midnight turned into bright midday. The rain abruptly stopped. As in previous crises, by the time I had started praying "Jesus help me!" the clouds had been replaced by beautiful sunlight.

Similar incidents have occurred in the past when I called on Jesus for help without even thinking—once when one of the motors on the plane quit; another time when heavy ice accumulated on the wings; several times in near tragic automobile accidents; and often in my medical practice during treatment of critically ill patients. We all seem to automatically revert to this innate subconscious awareness of God when catastrophe occurs.

Gladys Hunt in *Don't Be Afraid to Die* summarizes this awareness quite well when she states:

> We are limited by concepts of time and space; we need an eternal point of view. Your reaction to death will be conditioned by your reaction to God. Those afraid of God are most fearful of death. They who know Him well seem to welcome the opportunity of being with Him. That's the dimension that transforms death—knowing God.[1]

In spite of our vast scientific accomplishments we still cannot define God. Believing the first four words of the Bible remains a stumbling block to many people. However, even before biblical revelations man knew about God. God left His mark of identity upon men when He molded man in His own likeness and the heavens have always declared the glory of God, as summarized in Psalm 19:1–4:

> The heavens are telling the glory of God; they are a marvelous display of his craftsmanship. Day and night they keep on telling about God. Without a sound or word, silent in the sky, their message reaches out to all the world. The sun lives in the heavens where God placed it . . . (TLB).

GETTING THE MESSAGE

The apostle Paul indicated that man has always known about God through inborn knowledge and in-

---

[1] Gladys Hunt, *Don't Be Afraid to Die* (Grand Rapids, Mich.: Zondervan, 1971). Formerly titled, *The Christian Way of Death,* © 1971 by Gladys M. Hunt, used by permission.

stincts, and that unbelievers will have no excuse on judgment day:

> For the truth about God is known to them instinctively; God has put this knowledge in their hearts. Since earliest times men have seen the earth and sky and all God made, and have known of his existence and great eternal power. So they have no excuse [when they stand before God at Judgment Day] (Rom. 1:19, 20, TLB).

In spite of this indwelling knowledge, man's acknowledged belief in the existence of God varies throughout the world. In a sixty-nation survey the percentage of those professing belief in a God or a "universal spirit" were reported by Gallup International. Those believing in the existence of a God were as follows: ninety-four percent in the United States, eighty-nine percent in Canada, eighty-eight percent in Italy, eighty percent in Australia, seventy-eight percent in Benelux (Belgium, Netherlands, and Luxembourg), seventy-six percent in the United Kingdom, seventy-two percent in France and West Germany, and sixty-five percent in the Scandinavian countries.[2]

Belief in an afterlife was claimed by sixty-nine percent in the United States, fifty-four percent in Canada, forty-eight percent in Australia and the Benelux countries, thirty-six percent in Italy, forty-three percent in the United Kingdom, thirty-nine percent in France, thirty-five percent in Scandinavia, and thirty-three percent in West Germany.[3]

India topped most of the nations in religious beliefs with ninety-eight percent of its people expressing

---

[3] Gallup Poll, *The New York Times*, Sept. 12, 1976 and Dec. 31, 1976.

belief in some god or a universal spirit and seventy-two percent believing in a life after death.[4]

Although the United States was rated as the highest in "religious beliefs" in the western world, George Gallup reported that the importance of Christianity in the western European nations appeared to be dwindling. Religious beliefs, according to the survey, were considered "very important" by fifty-six percent of the persons polled in the United States, thirty-six percent in Italy and Canada, twenty-six percent in the Benelux countries, twenty-five percent in Australia, twenty-three percent in the United Kingdom, twenty-two percent in France, and seventeen percent in West Germany and the Scandinavian nations.[5] A majority of people in the free world believe in a life after death. On the other hand, the official philosophy of the communistic countries embraces atheism during life and accepts the idea of oblivion after death.

CHOOSING TO BELIEVE

How and what man chooses to believe is indeed a strange phenomenon. Man will select one thing to believe but not something else, even when either belief may seem absurdly ridiculous on the surface of it, one as much as the other. By way of illustration, imagine your social club inviting a guest lecturer to speak. Your interest and belief in the message might vary considerably depending, let's say, on whether he were a journalist, an astrophysicist, or a minister. The subject being presented and the person presenting it might also influence your reception and belief.

For instance, let's assume a journalist is now talking to you about man's walk on the moon. Do you think

---

[4] *Ibid.*
[5] *Ibid.*

you would believe him if he showed you pictures of astronauts implanting the American flag on the moon's surface? Would you believe the moon is composed of lifeless dust and rock and that nothing else exists there? Or would you think the whole thing was a journalistic hoax? You would probably believe such a story if you live in America and saw the television news coverage of the moon walk, but suppose you have no communication by television or newspaper and are living in a poverty-stricken area of India. Would you still believe the story?

Now let's assume an astrophysicist, an expert in the realm of space exploration, is your guest lecturer. Let's suppose he tells you the universe is composed of billions of stars grouped into countless numbers of galaxies. Just one of these galaxies, he says, is our Milky Way, containing our own solar system as an insignificant part, with our earth not much bigger than a grain of sand by comparison. Suppose he says our own galaxy—our own Milky Way—is so overpopulated with stars that there are thirty-three stars for every individual living here on earth! Suppose he tells you that if man could discover how to travel as fast as the speed of light, 186,000 miles per second (so far man has only accomplished the speed required to escape the gravitational pull of the earth—about five miles per second), it would still take over 100,000 years to get from one end of our Milky Way to the other. Would you believe any of this?

Suppose this astrophysicist further tells you there is a "black hole" (or black star) in our Milky Way, similar to those contained in many other galaxies, where gravitational pull is so severe that time is lost in its periphery and even light cannot be emitted (appearing black). Instead of light, deadly X rays are discharged. Furthermore, he says, this black hole has such tremendous gravitational pull that it sucks up other stars like a vacuum cleaner, and therefore it is increasing in size and mass and will eventually explode. This great explosion will be initiated by the penetrating force of the smallest particle of matter known, the "neutrino." Would you believe any of this? You should actually believe all of it! This is supposedly the latest of scientific theories and observations.

Let's assume, as our last example, that your guest lecturer is a minister. Would that immediately turn you off? Let's also assume that he tells you God created the heavens and the earth. Nothing exists that He didn't make. Would that sound any more ridiculous than the "Black Hole" or "Big Bang" theories or any more ridiculous than saying everything came into existence by itself? If God did create all of these billions of stars and planets, why did He love the world, this insignificant speck in the universe, so much that He singled it out to have life? Furthermore, why would God give the earth all of the necessities for maintaining life—oxygen, chlorophyll, and water—so that life still appears to be unique to our planet? More wonderfully unique is that God went much further than this: "For God so loved the world, that He gave His only begotten Son, that whoever believes in Him should not perish, but have eternal life" (John 3:16). Do you believe this? Is there some reason that life everlasting is available to us?

Of the three examples of lectures I have mentioned, why do you think some people will believe in the possibility of the first two but totally disregard the third? Is it because faith in Jesus Christ is *socially* unacceptable? Would you feel embarrassed if someone discovered you were a believer? If you are not a believer, wouldn't the purpose of your own life be worth finding out about? What have you got to lose? If you *really* want to find out, here is a challenge for perseverance:

128

"Ask, and it shall be given you; seek, and you shall find; knock, and it shall be opened to you" (Matt. 7:7).

EXACTLY WHAT'S OUT THERE?

While probing the strange and wonderful mystery of why there is life on earth, we should also remember that God is still busy out there in the universe creating new stars and removing old ones, as suggested in Psalm 102:25,26 and Hebrews 1:10–12. He apparently is not idle, but continually building and creating, although the details of His creative activities are not clear. The Scriptures indicate, however, that Jesus is presently building heavenly homes for His "planned community" of believers and when He is finished, He will come back specifically to take these people with Him (see John 14:2). If heaven actually exists as a composite matter somewhere in the universe today—and I'm not sure we should conjecture—then we might assume there could be life on some other planet or heavenly body.

Those resuscitated people who seem to have broken through the "barrier" and claim to have glimpsed into heaven are most emphatic that it is a real place, made of solid matter, with streets of gold, closely resembling the description of the new Jerusalem in Revelation 21:18–23 (although some of them had never read these passages previously):

> The city itself was pure transparent gold, like glass! The wall was made of jasper, and was built on twelve layers of foundation stones inlaid with gems. . . . The twelve gates were made of pearls —each gate from a single pearl! And the main street was pure, transparent gold, like glass. No temple could be seen in the city for the Lord God Almighty and the Lamb are worshiped in it everywhere. And the city has no need of sun or moon

to light it, for the glory of God and of the Lamb
illuminate it (TLB).

If heaven is in existence now, I've often wondered
what type of transportation could ever get us there.
Even at the speed of light it would surely take too long.
Perhaps at the speed of thought? The Scriptures are silent on the subject. Nevertheless, it is interesting that
the people who have experienced life after death tell us
that travel is often at the speed of thought, that is, occurring instantaneously. Perhaps Philip's experience in
the Bible could be an example of instantaneous transportation. You recall that at one moment he was baptizing
the eunuch from Ethiopia in water somewhere near the
Gaza desert, and in the next instant he was "caught
away," or translated, and found himself in a city near
the coast (see Acts 8:26–40).

Having developed the attitude that the world be-
longs to us and owes us a living, we continue to waste
our lives seeking momentary pleasures. We consider our
food, our fuel, our shelter, and our clothing as our
"rights." We seldom pause to contemplate where they
all came from and how they got there. Nor do we give
thanks for them. Consider ordinary grass, for instance.
How did it get there and why is it green instead of pur-
ple or yellow or some other color? We are told that all
foliage is green because it is made of chlorophyll, a
green chemical. Then where did chlorophyll come from?
Was it inventively created or did it evolve from nothing? Was it accidentally manufactured from the pri-
mordial "ooze"? If so, man, being more intelligent than
the "ooze" should be able to make it. But he can't. In
spite of all we know, chlorophyll, that chemical sub-
stance that makes grass green, is still a mystery. If we
could just manufacture this compound, the world's food
problems would be solved! Chlorophyll makes our food
substances. In the presence of sunlight, it converts water

and the carbon dioxide we exhale into starches and sugars. This starch from chlorophyll, contained in the greens of all foliage and most produce, is the food of both man and animal.

It has been estimated that a chlorophyll factory half the size of a football field could manufacture enough food to feed all of the population of the earth forever. Now, if we only knew how to synthesize chlorophyll! Evolutionists imply that the "ooze" knew how to make it. The Bible suggests that only God can make it. Man admits he does not know how to make it. Should we, therefore, seek after the wisdom of the impersonal "ooze" or of the personal God?

BUSY . . . BUT NOT TOO BUSY!

While God is still busy out there in the universe, He, amazingly, is still not too busy to know me! To know me *personally*, that is!

During the trying times of my investigations into these life-after-death matters, I was awakened one night by a most unusual vision. Nothing like this had ever happened to me before. I saw a peculiar kaleidoscopic view of myself as a tiny image lost among thousands of fans crowding a football stadium. It made me realize who I really am in this world—nobody! Then it occurred to me, as I zoomed down upon myself, that I was now seeing myself as God must see me. I was getting bigger and bigger, and I began to realize that He could *really* see me. He was able to know me personally—and to know what I was doing. "Wow," I thought, I really *am* important after all! To me, I looked little; to Him, I could be seen at close range.

Having made me, He knows me and my every deed and my every thought. He even knows the very number of hairs on my head—and that the number is steadily going down! Jesus said, "Not one sparrow

(What do they cost? Two for a penny?) can fall to the ground without your Father knowing it. And the very hairs of your head are all numbered. So don't worry! You are far more valuable to Him than many sparrows" (Matt. 10:29–31, TLB). Thank God, He is not too busy to know me!

But am I too busy to know Him? I don't mean to know all about Him intellectually. I mean to know Him *personally!* I spent most of my life as one of the ninety percent of church people who are intellectual Christians but who don't know Jesus personally. Are you one of them?

10

MAKING SURE

Since embarking on my intensive personal study of life after death and trying to correlate what my patients report to me with what God revealed in the Bible, it seems that most every group I encounter soon loses its complacency and decides to take a definite stand for or against "life after death" as a concept, and also for or against Jesus Christ as the Son of God. Some stormy events have occurred and I am not always well received, especially when I bring up the subject of Jesus Christ in public.

Let me tell you how I see things in my present travels as a "new creature in Christ," going about giving talks to various business and church groups concerning retrieval of these victims from death and what they tell me of a life beyond. The interest is terrific. But frankly the condition, the state of the union, of many churches is astoundingly poor.

THREE OBSERVATIONS

First, I notice that many Christians, instead of becoming disciples of Jesus Christ, have gradually become products only of their own church doctrine. Don't get me wrong—Christ established the church and fellowship with other believers is not optional. But the attitude has become, "If you don't believe what I believe, you're not a real Christian," or "My church is the only *true* church."

It seems to me many of us are deceived; we are worshipping the church and not its Redeemer. Legalistically, we try to follow the letter of the law but in doing so miss its whole purpose.

It is also interesting that of all the resuscitated patients I have interviewed, none has reported being asked during the after-death experience what church he attended or what denomination he followed. It didn't matter whether they believed the soul was nonexistent, dead, asleep, or forever alive—this seemed to have no relationship to their accountability or welfare. Nor did it matter what they ate, how they dressed, nor where they worshiped. Although the accounts I have collected are incomplete, any preliminary judgment seems to have been based on one's own relationship to Jesus Christ and nothing more.

Secondly, it seems that overzealous scriptural authorities miss the beauty of their message by trying to overrefine the purity of the Word. Perhaps they should be called the "dissectors of the Word." They use the Bible as a cadaver, peering into its message for core words, often with a knife of mere human wisdom, cutting the Holy Spirit right out of the content. Their gospel, then, becomes like a flower without petals, a butterfly without wings, or a diamond without a setting. Holiness without heart is like a cross without Christ. Our main purpose as Christians is to glorify God in spirit and in truth, but without love this avails nothing.

Thirdly, I notice we all tend to keep Christ to ourselves. As we continue to foster divisions in the true church with legalistic tangents diverting the main theme, millions of our friends are traveling down life's highway with no road map and without progress. Some of them rely upon tranquilizers to alleviate the chronic despondency that underlies the momentary pleasures. During life's sojourn the ubiquitous rainbow of happiness continues to elude their grasp. They are not seeking God first. They seek temporary pleasures and blame their unhappiness on circumstances and other people they might encounter along the way. Real joy, the Scriptures indicate, is a gift of God and should not depend on circumstances or people. The truth is, people can be unhappy only when God is not in control of their lives.

MIRROR, MIRROR . . .

Along my own life's highway, I can remember many times when I changed my principles to suit my desires. Thus, pleasures could be fulfilled without them bothering my conscience. I adjusted my thoughts to justify my actions. I would pick and choose Scriptures that supported my beliefs without noticing the context of those verses. Intellectually I was indeed a Christian, while in my heart I was in fact a hypocrite. By self-deception I could continue the pleasures of sinning.

One morning several years ago in the Pentagon dispensary, I remember being called upon to remove several moles from the back of General George C. Marshall. Since I was personal physician to the Joint Chiefs of Staff and treated all the hierarchy, I felt inflated—I could do no wrong. Unfortunately, three days after I had removed the moles, they all became infected! As an Army captain, I could see myself being demoted to enlisted status and sent overseas. "Imagine a doctor attending patients as a buck private," I thought.

Then I began thinking of excuses that might justify the existent infection. Like, "Why was I assigned to do this kind of surgery since I am a cardiologist?" Then I began to adjust my principles to justify my actions, to explain away my predicament. "Any patient," I assured myself, "would consider it a *favor* if a specialist like me should treat a condition outside of that specialty purely as a convenience to the patient. After all, I had done so many times for my other generals (one of whom became the president of the United States)."

Fortunately, however, I needed no excuses. Always the gentleman, General Marshall evaporated my defenses with his kindness. He let me know I was still his physician. He taught me a lesson in principles when I had wandered off the course.

The Book of Isaiah tells us there is a highway of holiness and that, "the unclean will not travel on it, but it will be for him who walks that way, and fools will not wander on it" (Isa. 35:8). God says if I am not on that highway of life—the highway that leads to everlasting life—then I am a fool. Only a few times in the Scriptures does God call man a fool. We should listen closely! How, then, can we find the highway that leads to eternal life? Billy Graham says,

> This highway of God was built by a cross. The Old Testament looks forward to the Cross and the New Testament looks back to the Cross. The death, burial, and resurrection of Christ is called the gospel—the Good News that God has prepared a highway. He has prepared a road. He has prepared a way out of this situation of despair. But you must not only acknowledge Jesus Christ as Lord and Savior; you must be willing to confess your sins and turn from your sins. For the love of Christ leaves us no choice, when once we

reach the conclusion that one man died for all and death for all has been conquered. Since Christ's love controls us and "since we believe that Christ died for all of us, we should also believe that we have died to the old life we used to live. He died for all so that all who live—having received eternal life from Him—might no longer live for themselves, to please themselves, but to spend their lives pleasing Christ who died and rose again for them."[1]

MAKING SURE

Do you know what the fate of your soul will be when it is released from your body at death? Would you like to live forever? God says all of us will live forever, but only some will reside with Him. You can be released from a doomsday existence by appointing God's Son, Jesus Christ, as Lord of your life and Savior of your soul. This is the Good News.

God loved you so much He sent His only Son, Jesus Christ, so you could know God as a Man, so you could know the Scriptures are holy and true, and so you could receive everlasting life. Since God is holy, the Bible tells us He cannot accept us in our present unholy state. We have all sinned against Him by not recognizing Him as our Creator and God.

But God provided a unique solution. He taught His chosen people the seriousness of sin and the required solution—blood sacrifice by that which is perfect for that which is imperfect. In the Old Testament the Jews were taught this concept through animal sacrifices. Then, at the chosen time, God provided the perfect and final sacrifice. He allowed His own Son to be the blood sacrifice in our place. This is the core message of the

---

[1] Billy Graham, "Highway to Holiness," *Decision*, Sept. 1977, p. 2.

New Testament and the exact forecast of the Old Testament.

We only need claim the blood of Jesus Christ to obtain salvation and everlasting life with Him. This is a free gift for those who want to accept it. It also involves obeying God. He tells us what He wants us to do through the indwelling Holy Spirit and the written Word.

The Scriptures tell us we will become joint heirs of all things with Christ and that we can spiritually communicate with Him. A beautiful reminder of our heritage and goals in life was summarized by Peter:

> You have been chosen by God Himself—you are priests of the King, you are holy and pure, you are God's very own—all this so that you may show to others how God called you out of the darkness into His wonderful light. Once you were less than nothing; now you are God's own. Once you knew very little about God's kindness; now your very lives have been changed by it.
>
> Dear brothers, you are only visitors here. Since your real home is in Heaven, I beg you to keep away from the evil pleasures of this world; they are not for you for they fight against your very souls (1 Pet. 2:9–11, TLB).

Shouldn't we acknowledge God now when it will be to our benefit rather than later when it will be too late? You see, each of us *will* acknowledge Him: "As I live, saith the Lord, every knee shall bow to me and every tongue confess to God. So then every one of us shall give account of himself to God" (Rom 14:11,12, KJV). What is Good News now will certainly be Bad News later, and what is a real bargain now will later represent a calamity when we no longer have the freedom of choice.

There is a peculiar apathy and moral degeneration

now occurring in America and it closely resembles the situation that led to the decline and fall of the Roman Empire as was classically described over two hundred years ago by Edward Gibbon. Although our American democracy has existed only one-fifth as long as the one-thousand-year reign of the Roman Empire, the same five attributes outlined by Gibbon as the cause for the fall of Rome are ominously existent in the United States today: (1) bountiful affluence and luxury; (2) a disparaging separation of the very rich and very poor, which encourages civil strife; (3) an obsession with sex to the extent of extreme perversion; (4) a loss of originality and creativeness in personal life and in the arts; and (5) the emergence of a welfare state dissipating the wealth and strength of government.

While Americans are enjoying their affluence, eight million people in the world need to be fed. One-sixth of the world's population consumes the world's goods, while the nonaffluent starve to death. This kind of injustice is creating a revolutionary class within South America, India, and Africa. Death caused by nutritional deficiencies takes fifty percent of the lives of those under age fourteen, and yet the fantastic population explosion continues. Education, cultural habits, and irresponsibility continue to separate the haves and the have-nots. Neither money nor revolution can correct the situation by itself.

Rebellion in morals and ethics is widespread. There are 1.3 million people registered as unmarried yet living together. Our television and movie media are offering an increasing number of films on sexual perversion and now seem to be approving films that desecrate the life of Jesus Christ. Many ministers of the nation's mainline churches are deviating from biblical teachings, further engendering a great falling away and apostasy.

The precept on the street seems to be: "If everybody's doing it, it can't be that bad." Satan, the great deceiver, is appearing in many areas of life as a false beam of light or as a prophet or as a new life-style, leading many astray. But we should remember that in the last chapter, God wins!

Are you like I have been—a Christian of convenience? For years I was a Christian only when I found it to my advantage. I allowed myself to become religiously indifferent, complacent. I really functioned as a "part-time" Christian. The great majority of church-going Christians I encounter appear to be much as I was. That is, they know all about Jesus, but they really don't know Him personally.

THE BIG QUESTION

Once a nurse asked me after one of my lectures on resuscitation what I thought of a course she was taking entitled "How to Die." It was supposed to help the student face his or her own death with valor and equanimity. She was actually trying to deal with her younger sister's recent death and how it might relate to her own life.

I couldn't think of an answer at the time. But the answer is really very simple and it works every time: Put God first in your life, and you won't have to fear death. You don't need to take courses. Jesus has already conquered death for you. You merely pass through death into another life. Death to the real you, the real person, never occurs. You merely vacate your body until the resurrection. You have nothing to lose when you bet your life on Jesus Christ! You're a winner, regardless of whether your body lives or dies! Don't gamble on your own limited concepts, because you really can't see beyond your nose.

Among the doctor groups to whom I have spoken, I've asked their opinions on two questions (everybody considers himself an authority on life after death. At least, each has his own answer): First, is there a life after death; second, is there a God? With few exceptions there have been two-thirds voting yes to both questions and one-third voting no. Occasionally someone says yes to one question and no to the other.

Similarly, I have informally polled some church audiences. Each person was asked to write down what he thought would be a good definition of a Christian. The majority of the definitions on these cards pertained to the *character* of a supposed Christian—his family life, fidelity, reliability, and "goodness." Only forty percent of the people defined a Christian in terms of a follower or a believer in Christ.

Certainly, being "good" is a nice thing, but that doesn't make a person a Christian, and it isn't the thing that secures eternal life. Paul wrote, "For by grace you have been saved through faith; and that not of yourselves, it is the gift of God; not as a result of works, that no one should boast" (Eph. 2:8,9). And Jesus said, "No one comes to the Father, but through Me" (John 14:6). Surprisingly, the poll showed that many church members are apparently unmindful of the Jesus requirements for Christianity!

THE REAL THING

Putting Christ first in my life was something I had never done even though I had gone to church all my life. I treated church like a social club. I would put on my best Sunday clothes and hope people wouldn't realize how dirty I was the rest of the week. Using a mask of religious hypocrisy, I tried to disguise my real nature. Most people considered me a man of learning, but I was ignorant of spiritual truths. I was a Sunday school teacher for a while, but it was the same as the blind leading the blind, because I was not a new creature in

Christ. I was the same old person. My life had always been barren, like the nonyielding fig tree that should have been cut down.

Do you say you are not like that? Can you honestly say you have never broken your covenants with God since becoming a Christian? Don't believe it! We have all fallen short. "If we say we have no sin, we are deceiving ourselves, and the truth is not in us" (1 John 1:8). Knowingly or unknowingly, in the flesh or in the mind, I have the *tendency* to continue to lie and cheat and steal and lust and covet and commit adultery! The Scriptures teach that we aren't saved from sin's grasp by simply knowing God's commandments. But we are saved through Christ alone, and He empowers us to do God's will (see Rom. 8:3).

You and I must renew our dedication daily. Are you still a sinner? Yes, of course; we all are! I was a sinner when I became a Christian, and I'm still a sinner. The difference is I have been saved by God's grace. Now I have the power in Christ to avoid sinning intentionally or knowingly, and I can confess and turn from my sin as soon as I recognize it. The Bible says, "If we confess our sins, He is faithful and righteous to forgive us our sins and to cleanse us from all unrighteousness" (1 John 1:9).

Every morning I renew my battle against Satan and try to put on the whole armor of God, because I can't win in my own strength. I say, "Lord, you know what a sinner I am. I need your help and your forgiveness."

Thoughts from the flesh still conflict with my earnest desires. This spiritual conflict may involve old habits, lust, greed, discouragement, or even hate. Sometimes the battle is fierce. But I'm able to do much better if I dedicate each day to God, first thing each morning. I say, "God, this is Your day. I set it aside for You. Show me what You want me to do. Here I am; I'm available." Something usually turns up that day for me to do—perhaps to relate to someone, perhaps to reassure the insecure or to comfort the sick in Jesus's name.

* * *

If you have received a message from this book and know you need to commit your life for the first time to Jesus Christ, you can do so right now by bowing your head and praying something like this:

> Lord Jesus, I open the door of my life and receive You as my Savior and Lord. I believe You are the Son of God and that You died for my sins. I agree with You that I am a sinner in need of forgiveness. Thank You for forgiving my sins. Thank You for the knowledge of life after death. Thank You for letting me know how important I am to You. Take control of my life and make me the kind of person You want me to be. I dedicate the rest of my life to You. Amen.

If you have sincerely prayed this prayer, it's comforting to know that right now God has forgiven your sins, and the Scriptures indicate He will never leave you. Don't you, in turn, ever leave Him.

If you are already a Christian but you have become lukewarm in your faith, why not ask God to fill you with the Holy Spirit. When filled with the Holy Spirit, you can have a personal walk with Jesus Christ; you can talk with Him anytime, anywhere, just as the prophets did.

This commitment will be the greatest thing you have ever done. Could there be any better way to assure the future of your own life?

Do you remember the dying patient who was in hell? Some day you may be the one your own doctor is trying to resuscitate! But if you have received the Lord

Jesus you know where your afterlife will take you. This new life is immune to death. A believer in Jesus can't lose on either side of death. As a Christian, you are safe, and it is now safe to die.

BIBLIOGRAPHY

Albrecht, Mark and Brooks Alexander. "Thanatology: Death and Dying." *Journal of the Spiritual Counterfeits Project*. April 1977.

Allen, R. Earl. *The Hereafter*. Old Tappan, N.J.: Revell, 1977.

Board, Stephen, ed. "Light at the End of the Tunnel." *Eternity*. July 1977.

Budge, E.A. *The Book of the Dead*. New York: Barnes and Noble, 1969.

Coombs, Peter. *Life after Death*. Downers Grove, Ill.: Inter-Varsity Press, 1978.

Evans-Wentz, W.Y., ed. *The Tibetan Book of the Dead*. New York: Oxford University Press, 1957.

Ford, Marvin. *On the Other Side*. Plainfield, N.J.: Logos International, 1978.

Gatch, M.M. *Death: Meaning and Immortality in Christian Thought and Contemporary Culture*. New York: Seabury Press, 1969.

Graham, Billy. "Highway to Holiness." *Decision*. Sept. 1977.

Gothard, Bill. *Institute of Basic Youth Conflicts*. Oak Brook, Illinois.

Hamilton, Edith and H. Cairns, eds. *The Collected Dialogues of Plato*. New York: Bollingen Foundation, 1961.

Hunt, Gladys. *Don't Be Afraid to Die: The Christian Way of Death.* Grand Rapids: Zondervan, 1974.

Johnson, C.D. *The Morning After Death.* Nashville: Broadman Press, 1978.

Jung, C.G. *Memories, Dreams, Reflections.* New York: Pantheon Books, 1963.

Kubler-Ross, Elisabeth. *On Death and Dying.* New York: Macmillan, 1969.

Kubler-Ross, Elisabeth. *Questions and Answers on Death and Dying.* New York: Macmillan, 1974.

Lewis, Gordon R. "Criteria for the Discerning of Spirits." *Demon Possession: A Medical, Historical, Anthropological and Theological Symposium.* Ed. John Warwick Montgomery. Minneapolis: Bethany Fellowship, 1976.

Lockyer, Herbert. *The Gospel of the Life Beyond.* Westwood, N.J.: Revell Co., 1967.

Maltz, Mrs. Carl. *The Texas Herald.* Austin, Sept. 1977.

Matson, Archie. *Afterlife: Reports from the Threshold of Death.* New York: Harper and Row, 1975.

Monroe, Robert A. *Journeys Out of the Body.* New York: Doubleday, 1973.

Moody, Raymond. *Life After Life.* New York: Bantam, 1976

Moody, Raymond. *Reflections on Life After Life.* San Francisco: Cameron and Co., Inc., 1977.

Myers, F.W.H. *Human Personality and Its Survival of Bodily Death.* New Hyde Park, N.Y.: University Books, 1961.

Myers, John. *Voices from the Edge of Eternity.* Old Tappan, N.J.: Revell, 1976.

Nietzke, Ann. "The Miracle of Kubler-Ross." *Human Behavior.* September 1977.

Noyes, Russell and Roy Kletti. "Depersonalization in the Face of Life-Threatening Danger: A Description." *Psychiatry.* Feb. 1976.

O'Roark, M.A. "I've Never Again Been Afraid of Death." *McCall's.* August 1977.

Osis, Karlis and Erlendur Haraldsson. "Deathbed Observations by Physicians and Nurses: A Cross-Cultural Survey." *The Journal of the American Society for Psychical Research*. July 1977.

Osis, Karlis and Erlendur Haraldsson. *At the Hour of Death*. New York: Avon Books, 1977.

Panati, Charles. "Is There Life After Death?" *Family Circle*. Nov., 1976.

Pollock, J.C. *Moody*. New York: Macmillan Co., 1963.

Rawlings, M.S. "Acute Myocardial Infarction." *Current Therapy*, Philadelphia: W. B. Saunders Co., 1976.

Raynes, S.H. "Post Humous Experience." *St. Louis Medical and Surgical Journal*. Nov. 1889.

Read, Hadley. "Conversations with a Dying Son." *Farm Journal*. Mid-February 1976.

Ritchie, George G. *Return From Tomorrow*. Waco, Texas: Chosen Books, 1978.

Rogo, D. Scott. *Man Does Survive Death: The Welcoming Silence*. Secaucus, N.J.: The Citadel Press, 1977.

Ryrie, Charles C. "To be Absent From the Body." *Kindred Spirit*. Summer 1977.

Sabom, M.B. and S. Kreutziger. "Near Death Experiences." *The Journal of the Florida Medical Association*. Sept. 1977.

Sibley, Mulford. *Life After Death?* Minneapolis: Dillon Press, 1975.

Swedenborg, Emanuel. *Compendium of the Theological and Spiritual Writings of Emanuel Swedenborg*. Boston: Crosby and Nichols, 1853.

Swihart, Phillip. *The Edge of Death*. Downers Grove, Ill.: Inter-Varsity Press, 1978.

Varughese, K.V. *Life After Death*, Makerbag, Cuttack, India: Ebenezer Publishers.

Watson, Lyall. *The Romeo Error: A Meditation on Life and Death*. New York: Dell, 1976.

Welch, Thomas. *Oregon's Amazing Miracle*. Dallas: Christ for the Nations, Inc., 1976.

Weldon, John and Zola Levitt. *Is There Life After Death?* Irvine, Calif.: Harvest House, 1977.

Wheeler, David R. *Journey to the Other Side*. New York: Ace Books, 1977.

Wilkerson, Ralph. *Beyond and Back: Those Who Died and Lived to Tell It.* Anaheim, Calif.: Melodyland Productions, 1977.

Zodhiates, Spiros. *Life after Death?* Richfield, N.J.: AMG Publishers, 1977.

APPENDIX

CPR

Basic Life Support
For Cardiac Arrest*

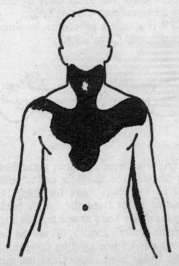

* Reprinted with permission. © The American Heart Association.

The most common signal of a heart attack is:

- uncomfortable pressure, squeezing, fullness or pain in the center of the chest behind the breastbone. Other signals may be:
- sweating
- nausea
- shortness of breath, or
- a feeling of weakness

Sometimes these signals subside and return.

After you have completed the training course in cardio-pulmonary resuscitation (CPR), you will want to refer to this material as a review of what you have learned until you take your next refresher course.

There are many causes of sudden death: poisoning, drowning, suffocation, choking, electrocution and smoke inhalation. But the most common cause is heart attack. Everyone should know the usual early signals of heart attack and have an emergency plan of action.

Basic CPR is a simple procedure, as simple as A-B-C, Airway, Breathing and Circulation.

AIRWAY

If you find a collapsed person, determine if victim is conscious by shaking the shoulder and shouting "Are you all right?" If no response, shout for help. Then open the airway. If victim is not lying flat on his back, roll victim over, moving the entire body at one time as a total unit.

To open the victim's airway, lift up the neck (or chin) gently with one hand while pushing down on the forehead with the other to tilt head back. Once the airway is open, place your ear close to the victim's mouth:

- Look–at the chest and stomach for movement.
- Listen–for sounds of breathing.
- Feel–for breath on your cheek.

If none of these signs is present, victim is not breathing.

If opening the airway does not cause the victim to begin to breathe spontaneously, you must provide rescue breathing.

BREATHING

The best way to provide rescue breathing is by using the mouth-to-mouth technique. Take your hand that is on the victim's forehead and turn it so that you can pinch the victim's nose shut while keeping the heel of the hand in place to maintain head tilt. Your other hand should remain under the victim's neck (or chin), lifting up.

Immediately give four quick, full breaths in rapid succession using the mouth-to-mouth method.

CHECK PULSE

After giving the four quick breaths, locate the victim's carotid pulse to see if the heart is beating. To find the carotid artery, take your hand that is under the victim's neck and locate the voice box. Slide the tips of your index and middle fingers into the groove beside the voice box. Feel for the pulse. Cardiac arrest can be recognized by absent breathing and an absent pulse in the carotid artery in the neck.

If you cannot find the pulse, you must provide artificial circulation in addition to rescue breathing.

Activate the Emergency Medical Services System (EMSS). Send someone to call 911 or your local emergency number.

CARDIAC COMPRESSION

Artificial circulation is provided by external cardiac compression. In effect, when you apply rhythmic pressure on the lower half of the victim's breastbone, you are forcing his heart to pump blood. To perform external cardiac compression properly, kneel at the victim's side near his chest. Locate the notch at the lowest portion of the sternum. Place the heel of one hand on the sternum 1½ to 2 inches above the notch. Place your other hand on top of the one that is in position. Be sure to keep your fingers off the chest wall. You may find it easier to do this if you interlock your fingers.

Bring your shoulders directly over the victim's sternum as you compress downward, keeping your arms straight. Depress the sternum about 1½ to 2 inches for an adult victim. Then relax pressure on the sternum completely. However, do not remove your hands from the victim's sternum, but do allow the chest to return to its normal position between compressions. Relaxation and compression should be of equal duration.

If you are the only rescuer, you must provide both rescue breathing and cardiac compression. The proper ratio is 15 chest compressions to 2 quick breaths. You must compress at the rate of 80 times per minute when you are working alone since you will stop compressions when you take time to breathe.

When there is another rescuer to help you, position yourselves on opposite sides of the victim if possible. One of you should be responsible for interposing a breath during the relaxation after each fifth compression. The other rescuer, who compresses the chest, should use a rate of 60 compressions per minute.

RESCUERS	RATIO OF COMPRESSIONS TO BREATHS	RATE OF COMPRESSIONS
ONE	15:2	80 times/min.
TWO	5:1	60 times/min.

FOR INFANTS AND SMALL CHILDREN

Basic life support for infants and small children is similar to that for adults. A few important differences to remember are given below.

Airway

Be careful when handling an infant that you do not exaggerate the backward position of the head tilt. An infant's neck is so pliable that forceful backward tilting might block breathing passages instead of opening them.

Breathing

Don't try to pinch off the nose. Cover both the mouth and nose of an infant or small child who is not breathing. Use small breaths with less volume to inflate the lungs. Give one small breath every three seconds.

Check Pulse

The absence of a pulse may be more easily determined by feeling over the left nipple.

Circulation

The technique for cardiac compression is different for infants and small children. In both cases, only one hand is used for compression. The other hand may be slipped under the child to provide a firm support for his back.

For infants, use only the *tips* of the index and middle fingers to compress the chest at mid-sternum. Depress the sternum between ½ to ¾ inch at a fast rate of 80 to 100 times a minute.

For small children, use only the *heel* of one hand to compress the chest. Depress the sternum between ¾ and 1½ inches, depending upon the size of the child. The rate should be 80 to 100 times per minute.

In the case of both infants and small children, breaths should be administered during the relaxation after every fifth chest compression.

	Part of Hand	Hand Position	Depress Sternum	Rate of Compression
INFANTS	tips of index and middle fingers	mid-sternum	½ to ¾ inch	80 to 100 per minute
CHILDREN	heel of hand	mid-sternum	¾ to 1½ inches	80 to 100 per minute

NECK INJURY

If you suspect the victim has suffered a neck injury, you must not open the airway in the usual manner. If the victim is injured in a diving or automobile accident, you should consider the possibility of such a neck injury. In these cases, the airway should be opened by using a modified jaw thrust, keeping the victim's head in a fixed, neutral position.

CHOKING

The urgency of choking cannot be over-emphasized. Immediate recognition and proper action are essential. If the victim has good air exchange, or only partial obstruction, and is still able to speak or cough effectively, *do not interfere with his attempts to expel a foreign body*.

When you recognize complete airway obstruction by observing the conscious victim's inability to speak, breathe or cough, the following sequence should be performed quickly on the victim in the sitting, standing or lying position:

a. Four back blows
b. Four manual thrusts (abdominal or chest)
c. Alternate back blows and manual thrust until effective, or the person becomes unconscious.

If the victim becomes unconscious, shout for help. Place him on his back, face up. Open the airway and attempt to ventilate. If unsuccessful, deliver 4 back blows, 4 manual thrusts, probe the mouth with the finger and attempt to ventilate. It may be necessary to repeat these steps. BE PERSISTENT.

INFANTS AND SMALL CHILDREN

To dislodge an object in the airway of a child, turn him upside down over one arm and deliver blows between his shoulder blades.

OTHER CAUSES OF AIRWAY OBSTRUCTION

An adequate open airway must be maintained at all times in all unconscious patients.

Other conditions which may cause unconsciousness and airway obstruction include: stroke, epilepsy, head injury, alcoholic intoxication, drug overdose, diabetes.

REMEMBER

1. Is the victim unconscious?
2. If so, shout for help, open the airway, and check for breathing.
3. If no breathing, give 4 quick breaths.
4. Check carotid pulse.
5. Activate the EMSS: Send someone to call "911" or your local emergency number.
6. If no pulse, begin external cardiac compression by depressing lower half of the sternum 1½ to 2 inches.
7. Continue uninterrupted CPR until advanced life support is available.

CPR for one rescuer: 15:2 compressions to breaths at a rate of 80 compressions a minute (4 cycles per minute)

CPR for two rescuers: 5:1 compressions to breaths at a rate of 60 compressions a minute

Periodic practice in CPR is essential to insure a satisfactory level of proficiency. A life may depend upon how well you have remembered the proper steps of CPR and how to apply them. You should be sure to have tested both your skill and knowledge of CPR at least once a year. It could mean someone's life.

EMERGENCY MEDICAL SERVICES SYSTEM (EMSS)

Any victim on whom you begin resuscitation must be considered to need advanced life support. He or she will have the best chance of surviving if your community has a total emergency medical services system. This includes an efficient communications alert system, such as 911, with public awareness of how or where to call; well trained rescue personnel who can respond rapidly; vehicles that are properly equipped; an emergency facility that is open 24 hours a day to provide advanced life support; and an intensive care section in the hospital for the victims. You should work with all interested agencies to achieve such a system.

SIGNALS AND ACTIONS FOR SURVIVAL

Know the signals: an uncomfortable pressure, squeezing, fullness or pain in the center of the chest, behind the breastbone, which may spread to the shoulder, neck or arms (the pain may not be severe); other signals may include sweating, nausea, shortness of breath and a feeling of weakness.

1. Recognize the "signals."
2. Stop activity and sit or lie down.
3. If signals persist, call your local EMSS number, or if not available, go to the nearest hospital emergency room which provides emergency cardiac care.

ABOUT THE AUTHOR

DR. M. S. RAWLINGS, specialist in internal medicine and cardiovascular diseases at the Diagnostic Center and Diagnostic Hospital, graduated from George Washington University Medical School. He is a cardiovascular consultant to Erlanger, Memorial and Parkridge Hospitals and served as chief of cardiology of the 97th General Hospital in Frankfurt, Germany, and physician to the surgeon general and joint chiefs of staff, Pentagon. Dr. Rawlings is a fellow of the American College of Physicians, the American College of Chest Physicians, the American College of Cardiology, American College of Angiology, American Society of Internal Medicine and the Tennessee Society of Internal Medicine. He was appointed to the American Heart Association's Council on Clinical Cardiology, is faculty instructor for the Heart Association's Advanced Life Support Program in Chattanooga and chairman of the local American Heart Association's Cardiopulmonary Resuscitation Committee. Dr. Rawlings is a past governor for the state of Tennessee of the American College of Cardiology, a member of the International Committee on Cardiovascular Diseases, clinical assistant professor of medicine for the University of Tennessee at Chattanooga and he is on the National Teaching Faculty of the American Heart Association.

We Deliver!
And So Do These Bestsellers.

Special Offer
Buy a Bantam Book
for only 50¢.

Now you can have Bantam's catalog filled with hundreds of titles plus take advantage of our unique and exciting bonus book offer. A special offer which gives you the opportunity to purchase a Bantam book for only 50¢. Here's how!

By ordering any five books at the regular price per order, you can also choose any other single book listed (up to a $5.95 value) for just 50¢. Some restrictions do apply, but for further details why not send for Bantam's catalog of titles today!

Just send us your name and address and we will send you a catalog!